Moctezuma II,
the Aztec emperor, certainly believed so.
This tragic mistake led not only to the phenomenal clash
of two diametrically opposed cultures,
but also to the turning of a decisive page in world history.
Bernal Díaz del Castillo,
Cortés' faithful companion and chronicler,
reported this crucial episode.

"We arrived at the Rio de Grijalva, which in the Indian language is called the Tabasco river. We reached it with all our fleet on 12 March 1519.... More than 12,000 warriors had gathered.... With great bravery they surrounded us in their canoes and poured a shower of arrows on us....

"Juan de Escalante, the alguazil mayor [chief constable], ...
was immediately sent [by Cortés] to Villa Rica with orders to bring ashore
all the anchors, cables, sails and other things that might be useful, and
then destroy the ships, preserving nothing but the boats.

"Moctezuma, the great and powerful prince of Mexico, in dread that we might come to his city, sent five chieftains of the highest rank to our camp in Tlaxcala, to bid us welcome ... he sent a present ... worth about a thousand golden piastres....

"When we entered the town [of Tlaxcala], there was no room in the streets or on the roofs, so many men and women having come out with happy faces to see us....
We marched into Tlaxcala on 23 September 1519.

"When [Cortés] came near to Moctezuma each bowed deeply to the other ... Cortés brought out a necklace of elaborately worked and coloured glass beads called *margaritas* ... this he hung round the great Moctezuma's neck.

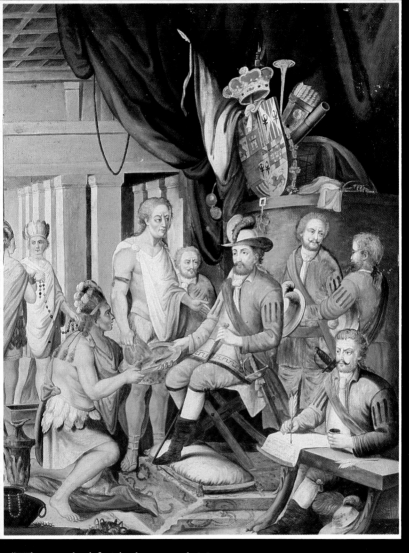

"When we had finished our meal, Moctezuma ... came to our quarters in the grandest state with a great number of princes, all of them his kinsmen.... The great Moctezuma had some fine gold jewels of various shapes in readiness which he gave to Cortés after this conversation.

"Captain Juan de Escalante, an ardent and vigorous man ... prepared the most active and able-bodied soldiers among those who were left to him.... He went off to face the Mexican garrisons. The opposing forces found themselves face to face at daybreak.

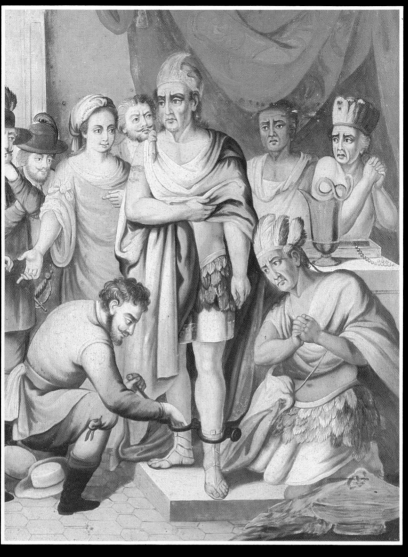

"On entering the palace, Cortés made his usual salutations, and said to Moctezuma: 'If you cry out, or raise any commotion, you will immediately be killed by these captains of mine, whom I have brought for this sole purpose.' "

CONTENTS

1 TULA OR THE MIRAGE OF CIVILIZATION
13

2 THE EMPIRE BUILDERS
31

3 THE AZTECS CONQUER THE WORLD
47

4 THE CLASH OF TWO WORLDS
73

5 FROM RESISTANCE TO COLLABORATION
91

6 THE AFTERMATH OF THE CONQUEST
109

DOCUMENTS
129

Further Reading
184

Chronology
186

List of Illustrations
186

Index
190

THE AZTECS
RISE AND FALL OF AN EMPIRE
Serge Gruzinski

THAMES AND HUDSON

cemostracion. delas. geulebas. donde auezauai.
los. mexicanos. mtes. delonqueistar esta
tierra —

deciendem. delos. bieje
me·los. gees. Una
generation. baleresa
dequescepien an como noso
tros. dlos. podersisos. Roma

For the first Mexican chroniclers who undertook the task of recording the history of their people following the Spanish conquest, one image constantly arose: that of the great city of Tula. It is to this image that they continually refer. Tula, imperial capital, left its mark on the entire history of ancient Mexico.

CHAPTER 1

TULA OR THE MIRAGE OF CIVILIZATION

Sixteenth-century picture (left), after Diego Durán, depicting the earliest stage in the history of the Mexica at the start of their migration, when they lived in caves and hunted for food. Man's head in stone (right) with eyes of pink mother-of-pearl encrusted with circles of pyrites, and teeth in white mother-of-pearl.

Since before the time of Christ, several sophisticated civilizations have developed, flourished and collapsed on the Mexican *altiplano*, that is, in the highlands of central Mexico. These civilizations were so wondrous that their memory survived until the time of Spanish domination. Two names are connected with them: Teotihuacán, the 'city of the gods', which reached its zenith at the time of the Roman empire; then, a few centuries later, Tula, whose ruins still stand some 90 km north-west of Mexico City.

Towards the year AD 1000 Tula takes over the heritage of Teotihuacán at the same time as it welcomes nomads and hunters from the northern plains

In the eyes of those who live on the *altiplano,* the Toltecs of Tula will always remain the initiators of all the material, technical and intellectual refinements of civilization. They are supposed to have been the inventors of painting, fresco and sculpture, the masters of the pictographic writing that covered papers of bark or agave with glyphs, the builders of magnificent palaces, the unequalled craftsmen of the mosaics of multicoloured feathers that decorated shields and adornments....

The Toltecs worshipped numerous deities, including the god Quetzalcoatl, whose priest of the same name ran his cult and governed Tula. The Toltec universe was far from being a completely homogeneous world: settled and nomadic peoples lived side by side, and successive waves of barbarians came from the north. They learned agriculture before being drawn into the

Toltec Atlas figure.

orbit of the civilized cities. Each group maintained its own organization, its traditions and its cults.

Yet it was in the cities that the technicians lived who built the dikes and dams that were indispensable to the irrigation of the land, and the specialists in the ritual calendar which marked the rhythm of everyone's existence. In the eyes of the Toltecs the ceremonies conducted by their priests were the only ones that could ensure the continuity of the cosmos and the gods, the return of rain and the growth of maize.

During the 12th century domination ends: the Toltecs migrate and disperse

For reasons that remain mysterious, the domination of Tula and the great centres of the Toltec period crumbled

The domestication of maize occurred several millennia ago in central Mexico. This vital discovery led to the birth of the first agricultural civilizations in America.

This part of the *Codex Azcatitlan* depicts the Mexica tribe during the original migration. The Mexica crossed mountainous regions where the vegetation was made up of cacti agaves, rushes, firs and palm trees, and occupied by *tequanimes* (wild beasts).

and then collapsed towards the middle of the 12th century. Doubtless the Toltecs could no longer absorb the northern barbarians; then the balance set up between

Camaxtli, the Tlaxcalan Indians' god of the north, of hunting and of war. He was venerated by the Mexica under the name of Mixcoatl.

the settled population and the new arrivals broke down, and migration became the only solution to numerous conflicts.

According to legend, tensions and rivalries forced the priest-king, or the god Quetzalcoatl, or both together – traditions differ on this point – to flee Tula around 967, accompanied by his followers. Some flooded into the Valley of Mexico, where they contributed to the foundation of new cities, which thus took over part of the Toltec heritage. Others reached Cholula, in the Valley of Puebla, or went as far as Chichén Itzá, among the Maya of Yucatán.

But the inheritors of Toltec culture were not the only people to reach the Valley of Mexico: nomads or semi-nomads of multi-ethnic origin, who spoke Nahuatl and Otomí, came down from the great northern plains and joined them, or forced them to share the land. Sometimes, several groups formed a federation: this is how the town of Chalco

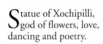

S tatue of Xochipilli, god of flowers, love, dancing and poetry.

I n the *Codex Telleriano-Remensis* the different phases of history are punctuated with calendrical glyphs beneath a date. The migrating Mexica tribe was made up of several autonomous groups.

Vitzilobuchtli   *otro hercules*   *Tescatlipuca. otro iupiter.*   *Tlaloc Hamacasqui. Dios de pluujas.*

Capitulo primero. fo.1   *Capitulo tercero. fo. ibidem.*   *Capitulo quarto*   *fo. 2.*

was founded; Chimalpahin wrote its history in the 17th century.

The Toltec heritage lives on through the reign of the 'god-men', who are in control of their separate peoples

The memory of Tula, a utopian model that was a perennial ideal, was a heritage as prestigious as it was unavoidable.

Towards the year 1200 the leaders of these wandering bands considered themselves to represent their protector-god, to the point of actually merging with him. These 'god-men' had bodies charged with the divine energy that enabled the *pueblo* (common people) to continue its progress and attain the goal that the divinity set it. In this troubled time of migration, peoples appeared in far-off sites and the start of their history is intermingled with the odyssey-like quest for a promised land.

These successive waves of population lie behind the extreme political fragmentation of central Mexico, where, up to and even beyond the Spanish conquest, there were dozens of tiny domains whose capitals were sometimes only a few miles apart.

During the 13th century the nomads assimilated what

Huitzilopochtli, god of war and the sun (above left), was the protector of the Mexica. His name means 'hummingbird of the south'. Tezcatlipoca, 'smoking-mirror', an invisible god (centre), was associated with the night and the north. Tlaloc, 'the germinator' (right), was the god of rain, venerated by peasants, and the 'lieutenant' of Paynal, 'the rapid' (below).

Capitulo segundo.   *fo.*

was left of ancient Toltec culture in the new towns. Newcomers settled at the approaches to these towns, having arrived too late to obtain any territory and being forced to settle in places that nobody else wanted.

For two centuries rivalries arise, each of the towns claiming to be descended from the Toltecs

Numerous alliances were made and dissolved between the new centres of power, and these excessively close neighbours constantly fought for supremacy throughout the 13th and 14th centuries.

Culhuacán, south of Lake Texcoco, had its moment of glory, being one of the only towns that housed a dynasty of Toltec origin. Later Azcapotzalco, the Tepanec town on the west bank, took over this role. Each leader, in either town, tried to link himself with the old Toltec line of descent. For a long time, Toltec – or more exactly Neo-Toltec – was synonymous with nobility, authority and legitimacy.

'Aztecs', 'Mexitin' or 'Mexica': a new group appears on the Mexican scene, already so well populated and full of history

Towards the middle of the 13th century the Valley of Mexico was entered by a new group whose origins are lost in myth and legend. Like the other ancient Toltec peoples, through a splitting of their origins, these Indians emerged from one sacred place but were engendered in another.

The story goes that this group came from the legendary Chicomóztoc (the seven caves), the mythical starting point for many of the peoples who came to the Valley of Mexico. For the Indians, Chicomóztoc was a symbol both of the northern steppes they took so long to cross, and of their original womb. But the group started off by leaving the mysterious Aztlán, a town built on an

According to oral tradition, the seven tribes who occupied the plateaux of central Mexico had a common origin. They came from a country located beyond the sea that surrounds the earth, or else from Chicomóztoc, the 'place of seven caves'. These 'seven caves' correspond to the seven tribes: the Acolhua, Chalca, Chinampaneca, Colhua, Tepanecs, Tlahuica and Tlatepotzca.

island, which foreshadowed Mexico-Tenochtitlán, or
perhaps was its replica in the past. Some believe that the
group was called Aztec from the very beginning, while
others see this name exclusively as that of the inhabitants
of Aztlán, in whose power these Toltecs found
themselves. Be that as it may, during their migration
they were given the name Mexitin and then Mexica.
The term 'Aztec', which was again adopted in the 18th
century, is now generally used to cover the peoples of the
Valley of Mexico from the time of the Triple Alliance.

Mexica

Huitzilopochtli, god of war and the sun, protects the exodus of the Mexica

Guided by its god Huitzilopochtli, who spoke through
the voice of his four bearers, the group undertook a long
migration through the northern steppes. The history that
was reconstructed afterwards is preserved in pictographic

manuscripts and, among others, by the indigenous historian Hernando de Alvarado Tezozómoc. This half-civilized people practised agriculture occasionally but lived mostly from hunting. It already spoke Nahuatl. In the course of its travels it underwent splits and disagreements, new bands joined it, and others broke away. Several legendary episodes evoke these wanderings, the outcome of which consolidated Huitzilopochtli's position as the supreme god of the Mexica.

The massive executions that were the finale of these events foreshadow the large-scale practice of human sacrifice. After arriving in the Valley of Mexico, the Mexica found they still lacked leaders of royal stock, and tried in vain to found a permanent settlement.

They lived for a while beside the lake, at Chapultepec, where they attracted the hostility of the people of Azcapotzalco (a dynasty of Otomí origin) and around

According to one of the versions of the migrations, the Mexica crossed Michoacán, 'land of those who possess fish', before settling at Tenochtitlán. Dazzled by this country's beauty, they consulted the god Huitzilopochtli and asked him to allow them to populate this place, even though it was not the one he had promised them.

1299 were forced to take refuge to the south of the lake, at the approaches to the domain of Culhuacán.

Here they were offered hospitality on the rocky stretches of Tizapan by the Culhua, who hoped that the venomous reptiles infesting this area would kill them.

No such luck: the Mexica roasted the serpents and ate them. Taking advantage of this break from travelling, which lasted several years, they began to become 'Toltecized'.

However, in 1323 they were chased off again. They were forced to penetrate the lake's marshes and reach an islet which marked the end of their migration.

On the plateau of Anáhuac, the Mexica found Tenochtitlán, the site of modern Mexico City

In 1325 the Mexica discovered the sign they had been waiting for. An eagle on a cactus showed them the site where they were to settle: Tenochtitlán. Shortly afterwards, a few miles away, they founded the town of Tlatelolco on another islet.

Nothing at that time distinguished this people of hunters and gatherers from the other immigrants; their tiny territory was squashed between the borders of the great domains that dominated the valley.

For thirty years the Mexica led an isolated existence, devoting themselves to building their two towns. Then they applied themselves to creating and developing the *chinampas*, those artificial islets whose cultivation requires such care and attention, but which, thanks to constant irrigation, produce high yields. But the lack of stone, beams and other raw materials eventually led the

The eagle on the cactus devouring a serpent – the emblem of the foundation of Tenochtitlán by the Mexica – is a late development. The 16th-century sources do not mention the serpent but rather the prickly pear, the fruit that symbolized the heart of sacrificial victims. This metaphor did not escape the Spaniards who replaced this evocation of sacrifice with the serpent (an animal more in keeping with the idea of evil) being crushed by the eagle, which appears in the coat of arms of the Habsburgs, the dynasty of the kings of Spain.

Mexica to emerge from their isolation and establish relations with the outside world.

The Mexica choose Acamapichtli, a lord from the surrounding area, as their leader

Acamapichtli was supposed to be descended from the god-priest of Tula, Quetzalcoatl, and in the eyes of the

Despite enormous technical limitations, the Mexica succeeded in carving impressive blocks of stone that they polished with abrasives, and used in the construction of pyramids and palaces.

lake's fishermen he embodied the prestige of the Toltec past. He remained leader from 1372 to 1391. He devoted himself to resisting pressures from Azcapotzalco, the Tepanec neighbour whose power had developed considerably.

The other Mexica town, Tlatelolco, chose a Tepanec prince. In this way the Mexica managed progressively to insert themselves into the network of alliances that united the valley's centres of power. Furthermore, a dynasty was founded at Tenochtitlán, and the many sons of Acamapichtli were to be the start of a new ruling class dedicated to monopolizing power in Mexica society.

The ruler of Azcapotzalco, a Tepanec called Tezozómoc, was the region's strong man at the time. Through diplomatic skill and military victories, he had

managed to build a true empire. A past master at the art of dividing his neighbours, he subjugated the region's different towns, apart from Texcoco, and hence created the most complete domination that central Mexico had known since the Toltec collapse, a domination built on the systematic exploitation of a network of marriage-alliances and on payment of tribute.

The *chinampas*, veritable floating gardens on reed rafts fixed in place with stakes, were consolidated by the muddy bottoms of the lagoon arranged in strata.

Under the tutelage of Tezozómoc, the Mexica gradually became privileged tributaries and were even able, with his consent, to extend their territory. Although still confined to secondary roles, they managed to take advantage of this period to train themselves.

Against the city of Azcapotzalco, Texcoco is the only rival capable of countering Tepanec power

Texcoco, so dear to Alva Ixtlilxóchitl, the chronicler who wrote its history, was founded at the time of the Toltecs and remained a town of secondary importance until the start of the 15th century. The north-east region of the Valley of Mexico received a large contingent of invading nomads, and one of their chiefs decided to make Texcoco his capital. Here, as elsewhere, the barbarian hordes knew how to adopt the Toltec heritage: they began speaking Nahuatl, adopted polite custom and wore luxurious clothes, while a group of immigrants from the southern region of Oaxaca introduced the art of goldworking and of pictographic manuscripts.

Gradually the city to which history would give the prestigious title of 'Athens of America' – but which was long ago eclipsed by the glory of Mexico – became a centre of refined civilization. Goldworking, jewelry, the cutting of semi-precious stones and featherwork mosaics were all such important and respected activities in the

This native lord is dressed in the traditional loincloth, the *maxtlatl*, and a cotton cloak, the *tilmatli*.

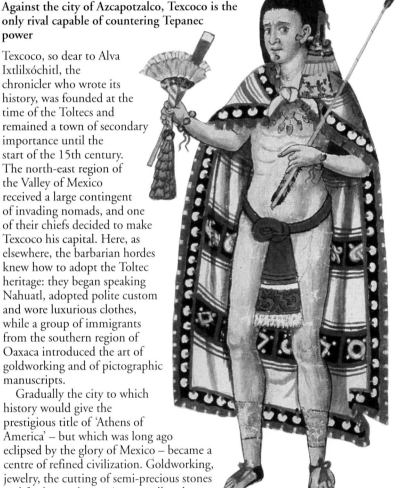

The 'Aztec empire' was set up in less than a century thanks to war and diplomacy, emerging from a confused situation in which the whole centre of the country was divided into numerous little independent states like the ancient Greek cities. Each of these states had the same structure of government: a monarch, assisted by one or sometimes several counsels, and surrounded by dignitaries entrusted with military or administrative functions. In all cases, the backbone of the Triple Alliance's domination was the tribute paid to the monarch by the subject towns. The lists of tribute indicated type and quantities, enumerating live birds, precious stones, maize, gold, pimento, clothing, bales of cotton and woven blankets.

Aztec world that even the noblest lords were not above devoting their leisure time to them.

The craftsmen who worked the precious metals, jadeites, turquoises and feathers were given the title of 'Toltecs', because the invention of these techniques was attributed to the ancient civilization of Tula and its fabled hero, the god-king Quetzalcoatl. They formed corporations that were grouped in their own districts, with their own gods and special rituals.

Tenochtitlán, Texcoco and Tacuba found a durable alliance in 1428: the Triple Alliance

So it was at the beginning of the 15th century, when Texcoco was starting to assert itself as a power of the first order, that Tezozómoc set out to clinch his domination over the Valley of Mexico. War broke out and, in 1418, the leader of Texcoco, Ixtlilxóchitl, had to abandon his city. A large part of Texcocan territory fell under Tepanec rule, while the Mexica were granted a right of inspection over Texcoco as well as part of their tribute....

Yet the empire built by Tezozómoc was barely to

Gold and silver jewelry was made (above left) using the lost wax process. The object's form was carved and engraved in charcoal, which thus served as a mould, on to which the wax was poured. The coating of molten gold or silver assumed the carved shape.

survive him. One of his sons, Maxtla, succeeded him around 1426. His brutality and errors quickly tolled the knell of Tepanec domination. The new leader of Azcapotzalco found Tenochtitlán and Texcoco in league against him. Nezahualcóyotl, the legitimate heir, re-established his authority over Texcoco, and, in 1428, Azcapotzalco fell after a siege lasting 114 days. The Triple Alliance of the Mexica, the Texcocans and the Tacubans finally succeeded in breaking Tepanec power.

The essential elements of the political scene that the Spaniards were to discover in 1519 were now in place. The Triple Alliance was to become the 'Aztec empire'.

The gold jewelry found in a tomb at Monte Albán – the mask of the god Xipe Totec (above) and pectoral (opposite) – constitutes some of the rare pieces that escaped the Spaniards' greed. While the Aztecs' clothing was relatively simple, their jewels and hairstyles were a mark of status and luxury.

In 1440 the emperor Moctezuma I succeeded Itzcóatl. A fascinating figure, generally seen as the founder of Aztec greatness, Moctezuma was only forty years old when he took over the reins of a fabulous empire. He was to be remembered as the father of the Aztec empire, but his reign opened with a series of terrible catastrophes.

CHAPTER 2

THE EMPIRE BUILDERS

This calendar (right) became the symbol of the Aztecs, almost on a par with the cactus and the eagle. The 'sun stone' depicts, at the centre, in a first circle, a human face with its tongue hanging out, traditionally interpreted as that of Tonatiuh, the sun god, demanding offerings of human blood. Opposite: Tlaloc, god of rain.

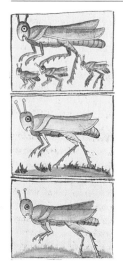

As soon as he acceded to supreme power, Moctezuma I began a campaign against the Chalca, who lived in the shadow of the great snow-capped volcanoes to the south-east of the Valley of Mexico. This war was soon interrupted by a terrible famine. In 1446 locusts devoured the harvests. In 1449 the city was flooded. A series of frosts and disastrous harvests cast a gloom over the years 1450–4. These events produced a wave of panic througout the whole valley, and famine raged for several years. According to the historian Chimalpahin, memories of vultures circling in the sky and of emaciated bodies wandering in the valley were still vivid in people's minds 150 years later. This succession of calamities showed up all too clearly the inadequacies of an authority whose power was based on extremely lax organization.

According to Aztec belief, the end of a time-cycle can mean annihilation

The leaders were swamped by the scale of the disasters, and abandoned the masses to their sad fate. This was the ultimate failure for a power whose very essence resided in the protection of the people. Aztec society was tottering on its foundations.

Luckily, in 1455, abundant rains produced an enormous maize harvest. But that year also coincided with the end of a fifty-two-year cycle, a crucial date marked by anxiously performed ceremonies: if, at that precise time, fire was not relit on the Hill of the Star, the world would disappear. The Aztecs believed that our universe is perishable, and that time consists of a

The chronological system of the ancient Mexicans was founded on the overlapping of a solar calendar of 365 days and a divinatory calendar of 260 days. Each day of the solar calendar was designated by the name of the ritual day corresponding to it. The year always started with one of the four bearer-signs: the reed, the sacrificial knife, the house and the rabbit. In order to make the two calendars correspond, these four signs were each combined with the thirteen ritual numbers (below), thus giving fifty-two years.

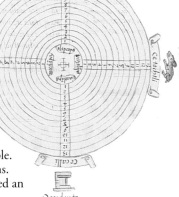

chain of cycles that were doomed to lead to annihilation. The world's destiny was defined by the date that marked its birth, when the sun began moving: *nahui ollin*. The twilight monsters, the Tzitzimime, who awaited the fatal hour far to the west, would rush to attack the living. But this time the fires burned again in the temples. The disasters of 1450–4 were attributed to the gods' anger.

Moctezuma I starts a perpetual war between the Triple Alliance and the peoples of the Valley of Puebla-Tlaxcala, who lived on the other side of the volcanoes

In order to appease the gods and to capture the largest possible number of prisoners, who were to become sacrificial offerings, regular campaigns were organized.

The passage from one fifty-two-year cycle to another was marked by an important ritual. At sunset the priests climbed to the temple at the top of the hill known as Cerro de la Estrella, or Hill of the Star, and waited for the appearance of the Pleiades. A new fire was lit in the open chest of a victim. Then runners set their torches ablaze and relit the altars.

fiesta delos ni[?]os a los [?]es dioses [?]ela n[?] dela sem[?]
lla y de y delica[?]/ aqui nacen [?]a
[?]r muger

Dios delos ni[?]os
el q̄ [?][?]a [?]a g[?]
en me[?]es [?]ol[?]a[?]
old[?] [?]ilto [?] [?]ola [?] [?]ell

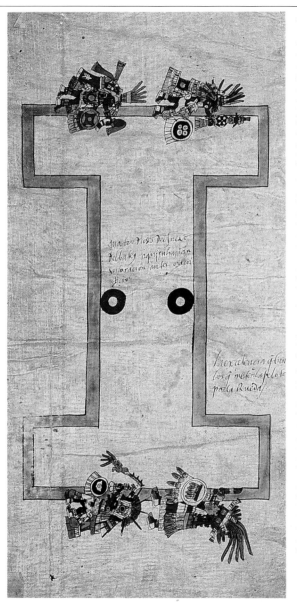

There were two to three hundred festivals per year, a crucial element of indigenous life; they satisfied the desire to integrate the individual into society by all possible means, and expressed different ways of conceiving and stabilizing time through the repetition of rituals. The ceremony called *xocotl* (opposite) took place in the tenth month of the year. The people holding hands are captives, dressed in loincloths and paper cloaks. They danced for part of the night and, in the morning, were sacrificed by being burned at the stake in honour of the god Paynal. The ball game (left), called *tlachtli*, is depicted in manuscripts by a double-T plan. Two teams faced each other, and the game consisted of passing a ball into the opponents' area by touching it only with the knees or hips. On the side-walls there are two stone rings through which the players had to pass the ball. Like all Aztec games, this one had a symbolic dimension: the court represented the world, and the ball either the sun or the moon.

The idea was not so much to conquer the enemy but to find offerings for the gods. This planned war was a huge game, a regular training exercise for more distant campaigns and a carefully orchestrated ritual aimed at making the gods and the world live on. It was given the name of 'War of the Flowers'.

It was not a complete innovation; it was probably the systematization of earlier practices known to the ancient Mexicans. But not every war declared by the Aztecs was a War of the Flowers: the conflict's ritual and cosmic aspects often overlapped with strategic or commercial objectives.

The most enviable fate, and the one closest to Aztec vocation, was to die in combat or on a sacrificial stone. By such means one would join the sun in his triumphal march. Young warriors became eagle-knights. This belief was the justification for a century of the large-scale War of the Flowers.

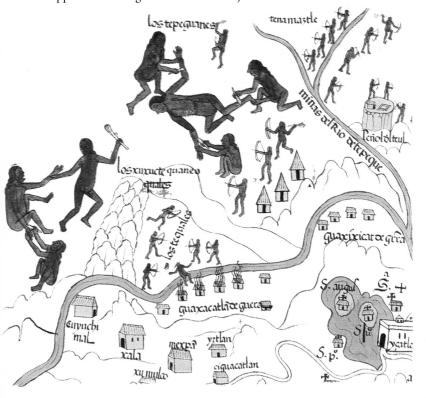

Be that as it may, from this point on hostilities never ceased to dominate relations between the Triple Alliance and the peoples of the Valley of Puebla-Tlaxcala. They lasted until the arrival of the Spaniards, who took excellent advantage of this particular combination of circumstances.

These hostilities were in keeping with a vigorous renewal of Aztec expansion towards the rich tropical countries that had taken in the starving refugees from the Valley of Mexico. The lands of the Gulf of Mexico abounded in feathers, precious stones, cotton and brilliantly coloured fabrics. Naturally these were all goods that the valley's nobles coveted.

Moctezuma I successfully sets out to conquer the tropical provinces

Moctezuma began by striking blows against the south-east, and in 1458 seized Coixtlahuaca, a city famous for its market. The key to the land of the Mixtecs – a land of ancient civilization, renowned for its painted codices and its goldwork – up the route to far-off Guatemala.

Moctezuma's troops then invaded the Gulf's eastern regions, forcing the Huaxtecs and Totonacs to pay tribute. In 1466 Moctezuma's last campaign was carried out in the countries extending beyond the volcanoes. Again in line with commercial objectives, the attack was directed against the city of Tepeaca, which commanded the routes leading both south and south-east. The payment of tribute, and the careful acquisition of strategic bases on commercial axes, all indicate how much economic preoccupations really guided the Triple Alliance's military enterprises.

In warfare the Aztecs wore special clothing. The uniforms of 'jaguar-knights' were tight-fitting. The warrior's classic armour, *ichcahuipilli* or 'cotton bodice', was a jerkin, padded to stop arrows from piercing the body.

The Triple Alliance's expansion is accompanied by a profound reordering of both Mexica and Texcocan society

At both Tenochtitlán and Texcoco, a complex etiquette henceforth marked the life of the sovereign and courtiers. One indicator of the progressive centralization of power was the fact that Moctezuma and his brother Tlacaélel enjoyed extraordinary privileges that distinguished them from the aristocracy. Rank was marked by adornments and clothing whose degree of luxury and refinement varied according to the wearer. Thus, bracelets, brilliant feathers, golden diadems and greenstones were reserved for the aristocracy. The wearing of cotton garments and the length of mantles were fixed by strict rules; any violation was punished severely. Although not unconnected to a preoccupation with elegance, these rules of clothing were, above all, signs of social status, aimed at differentiating common people from hereditary nobility.

However, it was not a closed system: warriors who distinguished themselves through bravery also received their share of honours and adornments such as shell or bone

Princes and dignitaries made great use of the sumptuous green feathers of the quetzal and the red and yellow feathers of parrots.

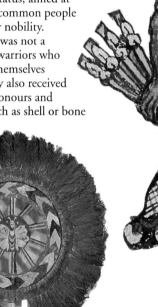

necklaces, and eagle feathers. The commoners had to make do with obsidian earrings and rabbit skins. These differences constituted a crucial feature of Aztec cultures: the conventions went beyond social distinctions, and were aimed at integrating the individual into society by every possible means, removing any personal particularities by assigning everyone a role, a visual character and, indeed, a definite image.

It was also in the reign of Moctezuma I and of Nezahualcóyotl, his Texcocan ally, that laws were set up that fixed systematic penalties for adulterers, drunks and thieves; punishments were especially severe for offenders from the nobility, as if it was inadmissible that those in power should set a bad example. Other measures were aimed at guaranteeing the integrity of judges. But these decisions only affected those from the regions of Tenochtitlán and Texcoco.

Featherwork, reserved for plumage specialists, was carried out as follows: a framework of reeds was covered with a screen of fairly ordinary feathers which made a solid base. The featherworkers always used the same method of fixing them in place. The feather's stem was reinforced with a thin bamboo tube, and then the feathers were fastened in little clusters using agave thread. The whole thing was fixed to the framework with a thicker thread. When this screen was in place, the same process was carried out with the precious feathers (quetzal, macaw, and so on), that is, their stems were consolidated, and they were basted before being sewn to the framework. The white down of the quetzal feathers (which were a golden green) was concealed with a fringe of pink-coloured feathers, which was then set in place on top. Finally, the whole thing was often decorated with precious stones.

The Triple Alliance's military expeditions display weakness as well as strength

The establishment of Aztec rule in these far-off countries was not a foregone conclusion: the Aztecs left no garrison behind, not even an Aztec governor in residence, except for an official whose job was to collect tribute and to make sure it was sent to Tenochtitlán. Apart from this, the Mexica and their allies respected local authorities, institutions and traditions. In any case, they had no regular army, apart from a military élite comprising 'jaguar-knights' and 'eagle-knights', who were too few in number to serve as an occupying force.

Although the Mexica sometimes imposed the cult of Huitzilopochtli, their tutelary god, they never bothered to proscribe the local divinities. The very idea of

The sacrificed prisoner was no longer an enemy being killed but a messenger being sent to the gods, himself invested with an almost divine dignity. When a man took a prisoner, he said: 'Here is my beloved son,' and the captive said: 'Here is my revered father.'

conversion was alien to the peoples of ancient Mexico, whereas it was one of the linchpins of Christianity.

There are further important obstacles to true control: enormous distances and rudimentary means of communication

The troops of Tenochtitlán and the caravans of tribute had to cover several hundred miles, cross mountain barriers and precipices, tackle almost impenetrable vegetation, or traverse cold and dry plateaux, before descending the tropical slopes that led to the Atlantic or Pacific. The difficulties they faced were all the greater in that none of these societies was familiar with either the mule or the horse, or used the wheel: everything had to be carried on men's backs.

It is therefore easy to understand that the local authorities were sometimes tempted to shake off Aztec control and, in a moment of exasperation, do something irrevocable. However, these spasmodic revolts only resulted in unleashing brutal reprisals which usually ended in the rebels being crushed and then subjected to even higher payments of tribute.

One of the emperor's primary functions was to command the armies not only of Tenochtitlán but also of the allied cities. Amongst the great dignitaries surrounding him, the most important people held offices that were, at least in origin, of a military nature.

The power of the tax-collectors, the Triple Alliance's only representatives, rests on the image it has managed to create for itself

The Triple Alliance's image was both that of a repressive power, founded on armed violence, and that of a more subtle authority, relying on negotiation as much as on terror, which was carefully maintained.

Thus, leaders who had not yet been subjugated by the Triple Alliance were periodically invited to attend the human sacrifices carried out in Tenochtitlán. Received in the greatest luxury, they could observe at leisure the way in which the victims – often their kinsmen, captured in war– were offered to the gods of Tenochtitlán. It was naturally out of the question to turn down the invitation, since any refusal would immediately be seen as a reason for starting war.

But the Triple Alliance also knew how to take care of the collaboration of the satellite populations of the Valley of Mexico and its surroundings: in exchange for their contingents, the Aztecs granted them a share in the war booty. More remote cities received preferential treatment, aimed at guaranteeing their loyalty. Others were entrusted with the guarding of frontiers, which exempted them from tribute payments.

This empire thus resembled an immense spider's web, with the Triple Alliance at its centre, and with a thousand networks linked together through marriage-alliances, exchange of services, interdependence and extortion. The whole thing was pretty flexible and always perfectly adapted to an authority that could rely neither on efficient means of transport nor on alphabetical writing, that instrument of rapid communication. In other words, it was nothing like a highly centralized and totalitarian power.

The empire is far from being subject to the rule of Tenochtitlán alone. Texcoco, its partner in the Triple Alliance, is no mere second-best

This allied city received the same share of tribute as Tenochtitlán, that is, two-fifths. It took part in the military campaigns, extended its hold over

At Tenochtitlán every man was a warrior. Only when he had captured prisoners could he reach the upper ranks and wear feather headdresses, and leather bracelets. He could then become a *quachictli* or *quauhchichimecatl*.

neighbouring towns and the north-east of the valley, and received tribute from the lands of the Gulf of Mexico.

Moreover, it exercised remarkable cultural influence, thanks to the activities of Nezahualcóyotl, a particularly brilliant ruler. Renowned as a legislator – he revived some laws of Quetzalcoatl, his Toltec ancestor – and as a builder and poet, Nezahualcóyotl had the allure of a renaissance prince with an eventful youth.

He was said to be descended from the gods, and to be immortal, qualities lacking in his ally Moctezuma.

At the end of his career a warrior could attain one of the two upper military orders: that of the 'jaguar-knights' whose war-costume was a jaguar skin and that of the 'eagle-knights' whose helmet was an eagle-head.

According to one of his descendants, the chronicler Alva
Ixtlilxóchitl, he even had the intuition of a supreme
god, creator of heaven and earth; the chronicler
enthusiastically called him 'the most powerful, valiant
and wise prince ... there has ever been in this New
World'.

For Texcoco and Tenochtitlán, payment of tribute forms the backbone of the empire

Brought in by endless lines of bearers converging
on the Aztec capital, tribute gathered
together everything ancient Mexico could
produce and
consume.
Several tens of
thousands of
tons of food,
more than
100,000
cotton
garments,
over 30,000
bundles of
feathers, and
an impressive
quantity of
precious
objects and
rare animals
constituted the tribute
paid in a year.
    Supervised by local tax-
collectors at the point of
departure, the tribute was
carefully counted, and traces
of this can be found in several
codices.
    The merchandise had
many destinations: in a
society that did not

Nezahualcóyotl
(1402–72), king
of Texcoco, a poet,
philosopher and talented
builder, was the most
refined representative of
ancient Mexican culture.

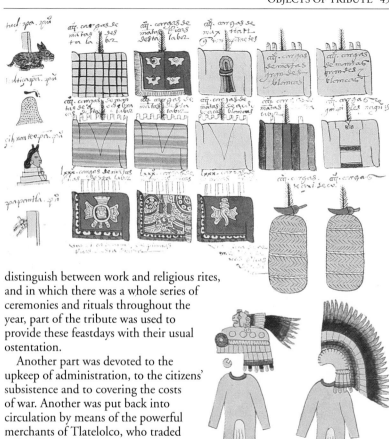

distinguish between work and religious rites, and in which there was a whole series of ceremonies and rituals throughout the year, part of the tribute was used to provide these feastdays with their usual ostentation.

Another part was devoted to the upkeep of administration, to the citizens' subsistence and to covering the costs of war. Another was put back into circulation by means of the powerful merchants of Tlatelolco, who traded it for other goods.

To the tribute were added the contingents of workers, with which the subject populations had to provide Tenochtitlán. These men took part in the great construction projects in the capital.

In 1465 Moctezuma undertook one of the last campaigns of his reign, and conquered Chalco after twenty years of war. He died shortly afterwards, around 1468. He had been the tireless architect of Aztec power.

The objects of tribute depicted above include (lower right) two lots of four hundred bales of dried pimento and a headdress of quetzal feathers.

In 1472, shortly after Moctezuma's death, his great ally, the poet-king Nezahualcóyotl, died in his turn. The Triple Alliance ended by merging with the identity of its illustrious founder. After him it passed to mediocre successors at the very moment when Tenochtitlán reached its crisis and turning-point.

CHAPTER 3

THE AZTECS CONQUER THE WORLD

The sight of human blood on the 114 steps (opposite) of the *teocalli* (in Nahuatl, 'house of god'), one of the two sanctuaries of the Great Temple of Tenochtitlán, horrified the Spaniards who had just arrived in Mexico. Right: 17th-century view of the city of Mexico.

The most serious crisis erupted in 1473 when Tlatelolco, the commercial capital of the Mexica, rose up against the twin city of Tenochtitlán, its immediate neighbour. There is little doubt that Tlatelolco, which obtained considerable wealth from the booty of the conquests of Itzcóatl and Moctezuma, tolerated the tutelage of Tenochtitlán less and less.

It had cause for regret. Axayácatl, Moctezuma's successor, emerged victorious from the confrontation, sacked the city and proceeded to deprived it of its autonomy.

However, Tlatelolco, until the Spanish conquest, continued to house an extremely active population of merchants who visited the whole of Mexico. It also kept its great market, the marvels and riches of which were listed admiringly by the conquistadors half a century later: gold, silver, precious stones and turquoises, slaves, cacao, ocelot and deer hides, game, tobacco, herbs, to name but a few....

Axayácatl repeatedly led campaigns against the west and north-west. However, these sorties continually ended in failure: the Tarascans of Michoacán proved to be tough enemies, as much of a match as the Tlaxcalans had been. Axayácatl's successor, Tízoc, scarcely fared any better, and died quite soon, bewitched by a lord of the Valley of Mexico.

Axayácatl's reign lasted from 1468 to 1481.

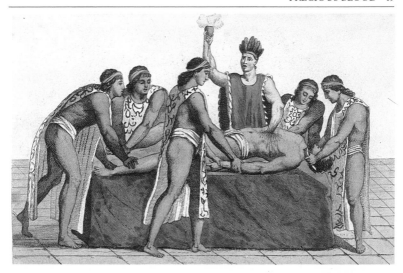

After two mediocre reigns, the Mexica again have a sovereign worthy of the empire and a strategist of genius: Ahuítzotl, the warrior

Ahuítzotl came to power in 1486 and began by leading several campaigns against provinces in revolt: they provided him with the captives required by his priests, since the work on the Great Temple, begun under Moctezuma I, was nearing completion.

The inauguration of this monument was the occasion for splendid feasts, as well as a tremendous holocaust. Some sources quote the terrible figure of 80,400 victims sacrificed in four days. Although this is probably an exaggeration, it nevertheless seems probable that several thousand men and women were sacrificed to the gods of Tenochtitlán in 1487. Immense queues of captives prepared for death converged from the north, east, south and west on the capital's ceremonial centre.

In ancient Mexico, human sacrifice (top) was an offering to the gods of men's most precious possession: their blood. The custom that most startled the Spaniards, ritual cannibalism (above) was in fact the attainment of a spiritual idea: it was a true communion.

CARTE DU MEXIQUE

Nort

Quincia
Lacus
Saltus
Tammanpul
Tanxira
Tammanpul
Tanapeguis

GOLFE

R. de Palmas

Tan Iacans
Tamcoca

du Cancre

Tropique

Tamaolen
delsa Ilaos
Tampaseo

Panuco
Tamaiac

Tempices
Salinas
Roxo
I. Lobos

St Filippe

Guaxanato

St Miguel
Concesion
de Salaja

Taxtlan
Xaxquohul

Tatletico
Aguatula

Tetpazapan
P Casones

MEXIQUE

Vila de Telagos
Macorija

Xacol de Ila

Volatica
Talista
Ostuma
Quecala

Cataculco

Nutatlan

Tzasuchtitla
Cacatlan
Ghales
Tlaxtla
Gua

Guernabal
Tentalo
Chouila

Puela

Acapulco

Puchuca
Achashica

MEXICO
Telaxo
Tzulepoque
Temba
Teracala
Zacotlan
Chiendritta

Cacere
Tlasala

Matalan
Xavaros
R de la Cruz

Antequera

Cfasla Xaltepeque

Llanos de Alberia
Nastlan Toluia
Almeria Terrebiance

Vilaresi

Cempoala
P de Sacrificios

St Ingalduia

Agaatulco

capellas
Tecapiepec

MER PACIFIQUE

Midy

Le grand Temple de

a de plus dans ce
blie à Mexique. ou
dies dans toutes
ou il y a des Com-

Ce grand Temple des Mexicains étoit consacré à l'Idole Vitzilipuzili c'est à dire le Dieu de la Guerre, & le Souve-
rain de tous leurs autres Dieux. Pour y arriver on entroit d'abord dans une grande place quarrée formée
de murailles, où plusieurs couleurs de relief entrelassées de diverses manieres imprimoient de l'hor-
reur, sur tout au frontispice de la premiere porte qui en étoit chargé. On rencontroit auparavant une espace

La pla....
liers étoier....
bitume ro....
oit l'Escalie....

Dances appellées Mitoles.

Idole de Viztzili p

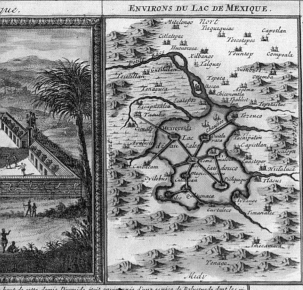

ENVIRONS DU LAC DE MEXIQUE.

On arriving in Tenochtitlán, the Spaniards were deeply impressed by the beauty, order and cleanliness of this city with between 150,000 and 300,000 inhabitants, one of the biggest metropolises in the world at the time. But this favourable impression rapidly vanished when they reached the great ceremonial centre. The immense enclosure, measuring 402.3 m by 301.75 m, contained several dozen temples. The highest and largest was the Great Temple. While experiencing the visual shock of seeing the bloodsoaked steps leading to the sanctuary of Huitzilopochtli, the Spaniards were struck by a terrible smell: the ceremonial centre stank like a charnel-house. These are French engravings from the end of the 17th century.

haut de cette demie Piramide, étoit environnée d'une espece de Balustrade dont les pi- les autres embar
quilles de limaçon & revetus de pierre noire semblable au jeais, jointe par le moien d'un les faites d'un s.
i donnoit beaucoup d'agremens à tout l'Edifice. Aux deux côtez de la balustrade à l'entrée contenir un homm
x Statues de marbre soutenoient deux grands Chandeliers d'une façon extraordinaire.

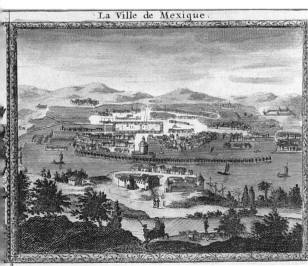

La Ville de Mexique.

Ahuítzotl himself, the sovereign, struck the first blow, surrounded by the leaders of Texcoco and Tacuba at the top of the Great Temple. When they tired of opening chests and pulling out the victims' still-beating hearts, dozens of priests took over from them in this endless, gigantic massacre.

It was a grandiose spectacle: in the flower-bedecked temples there was non-stop singing and dancing; sacrificers and victims wore the sumptuous adornments of the gods whose presence on earth they thus demonstrated. Blood flowed down the walls and the pyramid-steps. It is not difficult to imagine what an unbearable stench must have been produced from the bodies and the entrails by these sacrifices. Alva Ixtlilxóchitl, the chronicler, wrote a century after the Spanish conquest: 'This butchery remains unequalled in history.'

The Aztecs did not invent human sacrifice; it was already practised at Teotihuacán a thousand years earlier

How are we to make sense of this extraordinary scene and the killings planned down to the last detail? The Aztecs sacrificed their victims on an unprecedented scale and appear to have been obsessed by the urgency of carrying out mass sacrifices. They were motivated by many factors.

By far the most important concerned their gods and the cosmos: their gods were mortal, so they continually had to feed them, regenerate the cosmos and help the sun in its daily journey in order to avoid, or more exactly delay, the disappearance of a world condemned to annihilation. It was also necessary to ensure that the rains returned regularly and that soils were fertile.

In addition, human sacrifice was an instrument of government, upholding a policy of terror while at the same time enabling the physical elimination of the most dangerous conquered people, that is, leaders and warriors. In a way, ancient

"It was forbidden only to kill the chiefs.... The lord prisoner climbed up there, and a long thin rope was attached to his instep. He was given a sword and a roundel, and the one who had captured him came to fight him."

Narrative of the Anonymous Conquistador
c. 1530

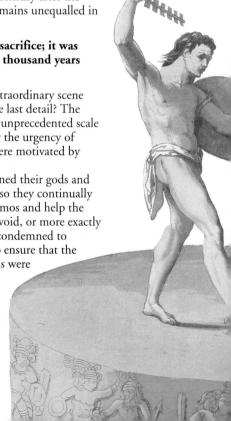

Mexican societies were 'societies of spectacle', with power expressed and exhibited not so much through a complex bureaucracy with many ramifications but rather through gigantic displays of the victors' inexorable greatness.

The grandiose staging of sacrifices has to be the reflection of the cosmos on earth, the display of the gods' presence here below and the exaltation of the 'prodigious' Huitzilopochtli

These countless killings constituted the source of vital energy, of 'precious water', that is, of blood, that was indispensable for the working of the cosmos. That effort had constantly to be renewed through colossal, minutely controlled rituals.

On these occasions, both priests and victims took on the gods' features. Indeed, they became the gods because the latter

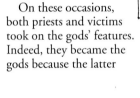

"He was cut up; one of his thighs was sent for Moctezuma's meal, and the rest was divided between the people of rank or relatives. They normally went to the house of whoever had brought the dead man into captivity. This flesh was cooked with maize."
Bernardino de Sahagún
Florentine Codex: General History of the Things of New Spain
c. 1580

literally entered the bodies of those taking part in the ceremony, man and god uniting in a single being, in order to allow divine power to manifest itself before the fascinated gaze of the crowds. The sacrificial victim was no longer just an enemy being killed.

Today perhaps, in a world where image and reality are becoming interchangeable, we may be better able to understand those societies that gathered together all their forces and resources to become a spectacle for themselves, in order to exist, to acquire an identity at the deepest level, and to delay the final cataclysm.

The annihilation of hundreds of human lives was, in its own way, a form of conspicuous consumption aimed at impressing subject peoples and neighbours.

The same unbridled lavishness, one of the essential aspects of the ceremonies, was also on display during the banquets laid on by rich merchants. A whole year's tribute was spent, or rather, invested in this way for the grandiose coronation feasts of emperor Ahuítzotl in 1486.

The priests threw the victim down on to the sacrificial stone; one of them opened his chest with a blow from a flint knife and pulled out the heart which was burned in a stone urn. The victim wore the clothing and ornaments of the god, and was called *ixiptla*, 'the god's image'. Above: an Aztec codex. Right: a 19th-century reconstruction. Left: the sacrificial knife was a sort of quartz stone in the form of a spearpoint.

War, tribute and human sacrifice are the pillars of a system that links the government of men with the regeneration of the cosmos

The dual necessity of reinforcing the Triple Alliance's domination and of ceaselessly renewing the food of the gods led Ahuítzotl to adopt a policy of non-stop expansion. Campaigns were restarted and intensified, first to the south, towards the hot countries leading down to the Pacific.

Exceptionally, colonies of Indians from Tenochtitlán were settled there, their mission being to develop plantations of cacao, a luxury commodity reserved for the nobility, and to keep guard over the frontiers of their dangerous Tarascan neighbours. The ruler of Texcoco,

"Its form [the city's] is square and resembles a chessboard because of its straight, wide and well-paved streets which correspond to the four principal winds: that is why one can see it in its entirety, not only from the middle but also from any position."
Giovanni Francesco Gemelli-Careri
A Voyage round the World, 1719

the wise Nezahualpilli, helped this enterprise with his advice, but from this time onwards it becomes clear that Tenochtitlán took the upper hand in military affairs.

Just as Christopher Columbus is discovering some of the islands in the West Indies, Ahuítzotl reaches Acapulco

Pushing on with his expansion, Ahuítzotl occupied the shores of the Pacific between 1491 and 1495. The conquest of the province of Oaxaca, begun under Moctezuma I, brought into Mexico a flood of rich tribute in gold, cochineal and painted cotton.

Further south, the Zapotec town of Tehuantepec became the Aztecs' goal. In order to capture this important trading centre, they set about their most distant expedition, causing unprecedented problems in logistics, administration and troop co-ordination.

In 1500 Tehuantepec called on the aid of Ahuítzotl against Soconusco, a country located around the present-day Guatemalan border, over a thousand kilometres from Mexico City. This was to be a very difficult campaign: not only was it necessary once again to release enormous resources to provide for the troops' subsistence over such a great distance, but the rulers of Tacuba and Texcoco came up with excuses for not joining Ahuítzotl. So he alone became head of the armies, and conquered Soconusco.

However, Mexica expansion ended here, because the Triple Alliance's armies were fighting on several fronts at once (against the domains of the Valley of Puebla, Huexotzingo and Tlaxcala). As the conquest-lists of each reign often contain the same town-hieroglyphs, there is every reason to believe that some of these victories remained precarious....

Chronicle showing the reign of Ahuítzotl (1486–1502).

While Ahuítzotl is constantly pushing back the empire's frontiers, the Valley of Mexico prospers

In order to tackle the problems associated with an increasing population, agricultural production had to be developed, and this meant carrying out great irrigation projects. Freshwater sources were diverted towards the lake thanks to this important work. But the ambitious operation ended in failure: in 1500, a flood destroyed the capital's houses and gardens, leading to their abandonment by the nobility. Ahuítzotl was forced to turn for guidance to his Texcoco ally. Nezahualpilli, son of Nezahualcóyotl, suggested that he destroy the aqueduct and appease the gods by celebrating other rites. In the end the strategist had to yield to the sage's advice. The waters subsided. It was decided to reconstruct the city.

Teams of workers sent by the cities in the valley were shared out among the noble families who made them construct elegant, brightly painted palaces, with splendid gardens and patios. Along the canal banks willows and poplars were planted; dikes were strengthened. The capital Tenochtitlán took on a whole new appearance, reflecting the empire's wealth and greatness. It was this new city that was to fill Cortés' troops with wonder when they discovered it almost twenty years later.

The flood served to reveal the tensions caused within the Triple Alliance by the power held by the Mexica. Ahuítzotl ordered the assassination of a lord who had seen fit to advise against the water conveyance project, and this cold-blooded murder spread consternation in the Valley of Mexico. For his part, the ruler of Texcoco, Nezahualpilli, took advantage of the catastrophe to dictate to Ahuítzotl and prove to him his supernatural powers.

Nezahualpilli secures the influence of Texcoco with the same talent as his father

Thanks to Nezahualpilli's wisdom, diplomacy and political skill, Texcoco retained an enviable role in the Triple Alliance. Like his father, he possessed immense knowledge and remarkable gifts: he is supposed to have

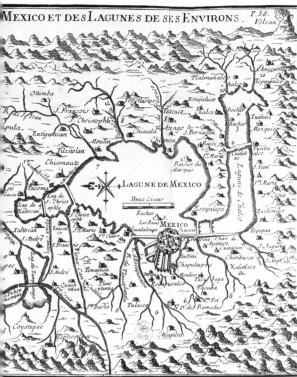

At the time of the Spanish conquest, the town of Mexico included both Tenochtitlán and Tlatelolco. This 'Great Mexico' was a recent creation. The town stretched from north to south, from the northern limit of Tlatelolco, opposite the lakeshore village of Tepeyac, to the marshes that gradually mingled with the lake. A series of named places marked the southern limit of the urban area: Toltenco ('beside the rushes'), Acatlán ('place of reeds'), Xihuitonco ('meadow'), Atizapan ('whitish water'), Tepetitlan ('beside the hill'), Amanalco ('sheet of water'). To the west it ended more or less at the position of Bucareli Street in Atlampa ('beside the water'), and at Chichimecapan ('the river of the Chichimecs'). In the east it stretched as far as Atlixco ('on the water's surface'), where the open water of Lake of Texcoco began. Overall its shape was a square of three kilometres per side, covering an area of a thousand hectares.

prophesied the arrival of the 'sons of the sun' (the Spaniards) and, according to some, to have escaped death permanently by withdrawing to a mysterious cave.

Domestic history, however, relates that he had a fairly uneasy private life: he had his principal wife executed. The same fate befell two of his sons when their conduct displeased him. He kept 2000 concubines who bore him 144 children. He particularly loved one of them, a lady from Tula, being charmed by her learning and culture. Among the Aztecs, polygamy was the privilege of nobility, but among royalty it took on proportions that justified the almost divine nature of the sovereign.

The empire's size begins to cause problems

Limits had to be placed on expansion: the Triple Alliance was based on the loyalty and goodwill of local leaders who were always left in place. So it by no means controlled the conquered countries, owing to lack of means and of men. Large amounts of territory constantly eluded it, like the domains of Tlaxcala and Huexotzingo in the Valley of Puebla. To the north-west and south-west, the Tarascans slowed its progress and sometimes prevented any completely.

Finally, since little integration of foreign populations took place, there was a constant risk of rebellion. The riches accumulated through conquest seemed to lead to a vicious circle: by stimulating the development of the valley and its

"We have already mentioned several times that the king of Texcoco, Nezahualpilli, had a reputation as a sorcerer or magician, and the most convincing opinion that I have found among the Indians is that he had concluded a pact with the devil."
Diego Durán
The History of the Indies of New Spain
1581

population, they caused an increase in demands and needs.

However, there is no doubt that the solidity of imperial power depended largely on the way in which the Triple Alliance's nobles and allies took part in the redistribution of tribute. In order to satisfy these appetites and this policy, it was continually necessary to launch new expeditions and each time they had to go to more distant places, making the sorties increasingly dangerous and costly to mount....

In 1502 Moctezuma II succeeds Ahuítzotl. Under his reign, power becomes resolutely absolute

Moctezuma II is the best known of the Aztec rulers. A scrupulous observer of omens and rituals, he was extremely religious, a trait matched only by his love of power.

Moctezuma II began by taking radical steps to change the way his ministers were recruited. The officials set in place by his uncle Ahuítzotl were eliminated and replaced by a select band of young people, all from the best families. So the nobility's monopoly on power was strengthened, while etiquette around the sovereign became much stricter.

Under Moctezuma II, the Aztec system was changed into one of absolute power, in which class privileges predominated. It was possibly thanks to these measures that the military and clerics reacted against the constantly growing influence of the great merchants, who flourished after the Triple Alliance's territorial expansion.

As for the outside world, Moctezuma II was to devote the bulk of his forces to subjugating and controlling unconquered pockets of land. Within the Triple Alliance's networks of cities and of tributary peoples, his predecessors' expeditions of conquest or punitive raids had often left gaps, sometimes even whole countries that had escaped paying tribute. The task was now to subjugate and absorb them.

Moctezuma II launched campaigns towards the south and the Pacific to subjugate the Yopis into the province of Oaxaca, to conquer the principality of Tututepec

The days of the divinatory calendar were designated by twenty signs: aquatic monster, wind, house, lizard, serpent, death, roe deer, rabbit, water, dog, monkey, grass, reed, jaguar, eagle, vulture, earthquake, flint, rain and flower. These signs always followed each other in the same order. Each of them was accompanied by a number from one to thirteen.

– a Mixtec domain in the ancient past – and to the north to finish off Metztitlan.

The success of these expeditions varied: the principality of Tututepec resisted some of the Aztec attacks; the Yopis, on the other hand, were conquered; and Metztitlan lost some important positions. Hence new cities located in the Gulf region had to offer tribute to the Triple Alliance.

Moctezuma II also set out to strengthen his grip on the province of Oaxaca, taking several towns by storm, and massacring whole populations. He decided to take these measures both to remove certain bastions that were thought to have become too autonomous and also to eliminate cities that were interfering with the flow of tribute towards Tenochtitlán.

The Aztecs abandon the ideal of the War of the Flowers

In order to crush their enemies beyond the volcanoes, Moctezuma put an end to the ritualized and balanced exchange of the 'War of the Flowers'. For a long time, the cities of Tlaxcala and Huexotzingo had been living encircled, cut off from the resources afforded by trade and access to the tropical countries of the Gulf of Mexico.

Salt, for example, was cruelly lacking in Tlaxcala, and the natives had to find and eat substitutes for this precious commodity.

Cacao, gold and feathers were equally rare. Since the reign of Moctezuma I, the campaigns against Huexotzingo and Tlaxcala had become more systematic, but could not really be called all-out war.

In 1504, however, Moctezuma II in his turn unleashed hostilities, taking advantage of a dispute, and waged war on Huexotzingo between 1508 and 1513, and on

MOCTETZOUMA XOCOTZIN.

Dernier Empereur du Méxique, peint par ordre de Fernand Cortez

From the start of his reign (1502–20), Moctezuma II, known as Xocoyotzin (the young), undertook to consolidate the empire by campaigns in those areas that lay between imperial tributaries.

Tlaxcala in 1515. But he suffered some stinging defeats and, at the time of the Spaniards' arrival, the results of his campaigns in the region were pretty mediocre. The Aztec war machine, so formidable in its distant expeditions, ran aground against Tlaxcalan resistance. A few years later, Cortés made full use of that unexpected ally's forces.

Thus, before the conquistadors' arrival, the Triple Alliance's influence encompassed almost 200,000 square kilometres and several million people. The population grew enormously, a dozen cities had more than 10,000 inhabitants, while Tenochtitlán had over 150,000, and may even have reached 300,000.

Great Tenochtitlán, centre of the Mexica-dominated world, focus of cosmic order, is ancient Tula reborn

It was therefore not surprising that, when they saw this unknown, marvellous city, the conquistadors compared it to Venice or the enchanted cities of chivalry-romances.

Although the Mexica undeniably held a supreme position in Tenochtitlán, their supremacy in the Triple Alliance was both contested and recent. It was challenged by the domains of the Valley of Puebla; and it was recent because it was only in the years 1504–16 that it established its position: it was in 1504 that Moctezuma II occupied lands at Chalco which had been dependencies of Texcoco, and in 1516 that he forced the Texcocans to elect his nephew Cacamatzin.

Despite this tendency towards centralization, the local dynasties remained in place everywhere, and no imperial administration was used to supplant them. Numerous, often tiny domains continued to function, and constituted the foundations on which the Triple Alliance's domination rested. The local dynasties were closely linked to each other and to Tenochtitlán through marriages and they frequently received a share of tribute.

The organization of government: power belonged to the *tlatoani* (the emperor), 'he who speaks'. The *ciuacoatl* organized military expeditions. The four dignitaries including the *tlacatecatl* ('he who commands the warriors') and the *tlacochcalcatl* ('the official of the house of javelins') were elected.

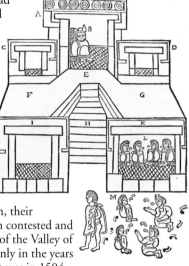

The throne (B). The palace where the lords of Tenayuca, Chicnauhtla and Culhuacán reside (C and D). The palace where Moctezuma lives (E, F and G). The war-council chamber (I). The council-chamber of Moctezuma and his counsellors (K).

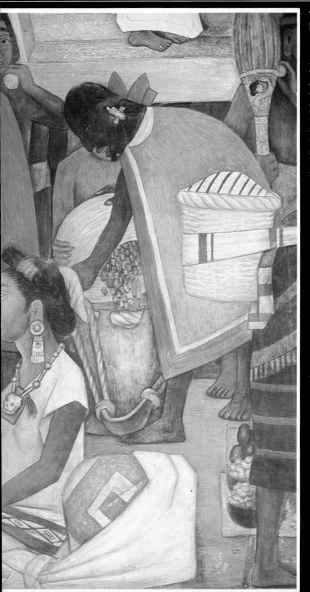

White maize, black beans

"And all food necessary to them also was sold separately: dried grains of maize, white, black, red and yellow; pinto beans; large beans; grey amaranth seed, red amaranth seed, and fish amaranth; white chía, black chía, and the wrinkled variety; salt; fowl; turkey cocks and hens; quail; rabbits, hares, and deer; ducks and other water birds, gulls and wild geese; maguey syrup and honey...."

Bernardino de Sahagún
*Florentine Codex:
General History of the
Things of New Spain*
Translated by Arthur J.
O. Anderson and
Charles E. Dibble
1978
Originally written c.
1580

Fresco by Diego Rivera
*Great Tenochtitlán: The
Sale of Maize* (detail)
1945

Gold, silver and feathers

"The ruler took care of the directing of the marketplace and all things sold, for the good of the common folk, the vassals, and all dwellers in the city, the poor, the unfortunate, so that [these] might not be abused, not suffer harm, not be deceived not disdained. Thus were things bought, or sold: they arranged them in order so that each thing sold would be placed separately – in its own place or station. They were not spread about in confusion. Marketplace directors were appointed to office. They cared for, and attended to, the marketplace and all and each of the things sold – the merchandise which was there. Each of the directors took care, and was charged, that no one might deceive another, and how [articles] might be priced and sold."
Bernardino de Sahagún
Florentine Codex: General History of the Things of New Spain
Translated by Arthur J. O. Anderson and Charles E. Dibble, 1978

Fresco by Diego Rivera
The Market of Tenochtitlán: Manufacture of Mosaic and Golden Jewelry under the Zapotec Civilization, 1942

Among the Totonacs

"The Totonacs occupy the northern area, and call themselves Huaxtecs. They have elongated faces and flattened heads. It is very hot in their lands, and one finds many foodstuffs, and numerous fruits, but no cacao; on the other hand, they have amber or the sweet-smelling resin they call *xochiocótzotl*. Cotton grows there, and they make mats and seats of palm painted in different colours. One also finds the other kind of cotton that grows on trees. The men are adorned with jewels and necklaces, wear decorations of feathers, and other gems. They are shaved in a strange way. The women wear elegant painted skirts."

Bernardino de Sahagún
*Florentine Codex:
General History of the
Things of New Spain*

Fresco by Diego Rivera
*Offering of Fruits,
Tobacco, Cacao and
Vanilla to the Emperor*
1950

It was like a sort of profit-sharing in the smooth running of the empire.

Under these conditions, the Triple Alliance's survival depended on the loyalty of a few dozen princes who, more or less voluntarily, made regular visits to Tenochtitlán, from which they departed weighed down with sumptuous gifts.

The political-geographical situation sheds light on the alliance's collapse and the sudden changes in public opinion that took place in the cities when the Spanish arrived.

"The city is so big and so remarkable ... much larger than Granada and very much stonger, with as good buildings and many more people than Granada had when it was taken."

Hernán Cortés
Letters from Mexico
Trans. and ed. A. R. Pagden, 1972

A few rebellions occasionally broke out, like that of Cuetlaxtlán where the inhabitants, annoyed at having to pay tribute, locked the Aztec tax-collectors in a house and set fire to it.

However, the native leaders were rarely dismissed, and were accustomed to a large degree of autonomy, and so they came to accept the overlordship of Charles V without realizing the radical upheavals it would eventually bring.

In the first decade of the 16th century, the emperor Moctezuma II thought he had become the 'master of the world'. But his sovereignty remained precarious, and the tyrant was fated to bow before destiny's infinite power.... A destiny that took the shape of a bearded white man: Hernán Cortés.

CHAPTER 4

THE CLASH OF TWO WORLDS

"His face, mournful and almost ashy in colour, would have been more elegant if it had been longer. The look in his eye was gentle and solemn; his thin, dark beard covered little of his face; his hair, of the same colour, had the cut of the period. He was broad-chested and had well-shaped shoulders. He had a slender body, with a little stomach and well-turned legs and thighs."
Bernal Díaz del Castillo
The Conquest of New Spain
c. 1568

The ancient Mexican Indians had a cyclical conception of time. The time of the gods dominated that of humans, so that, at regular intervals, divine forces came and left their imprint on human existence. Thus, certain conjunctions of forces, coming together in the same way each time, and certain past events were repeated whenever the same divine influences occurred together. In this way it was possible to predict the future, a task that was the privilege of specialized priests who checked the calendar-codices. Careful interpretation of wonders, visions and dreams could produce particularly valuable information.

"Ten years before the Spaniards came, an evil omen first appeared in the heavens. It was like a tongue of fire, a flame, the light of dawn. It seemed to rain down in small droplets, as if it were piercing the sky."
Bernardino de Sahagún
Florentine Codex: General History of the Things of New Spain
c. 1580

Growing anxieties: increasing numbers of signs seem to announce a gloomy destiny for Aztec power

The ancient Mexicans were extremely preoccupied by the day-to-day emergence of malevolent non-human forces, looming outside the ritualized framework of the relationship between humans and gods. In this respect, the decade before the Spaniards' arrival produced plenty of reasons to be fearful. Ten years before the coming of Cortés, a dazzling comet appeared. The soothsayers proved incapable of interpreting this phenomenon. Moctezuma condemned them to death by starvation. Nezahualpilli, ruler of Texcoco, who possessed the gift of second sight, prophesied calamities which were to destroy the kingdoms. When he died in 1515, he left behind a perplexed and troubled Moctezuma.

Other marvels came and sowed the seeds of anxiety in the Aztec ruler's mind. The sanctuary of the great goddess Toci caught fire. The lake's water formed gigantic waves, despite the fact that there was no wind. Women's voices in the night announced death and destruction. An enormous stone began to speak and proclaim the fall of Moctezuma, but defied attempts to transport it to Mexico.

The bewildered sovereign thought at one point of seeking refuge in Cincalco, the paradise of eternal life.

Below: the god Cipactonal (left) and his wife Oxomoco, in a cave, are busy devising the divinatory calendar, the *tonalamatl*. This picture is taken from the *Codex Borbonicus*, one of the most perfect Aztec codices, both for its content (calendar and ritual of the feastdays celebrated by the Aztecs) and for the quality of its paintings and their conservation.

At the last minute he was prevented from doing so by his entourage. He was only a simple mortal after all. Plunged into a state of extreme agitation, Moctezuma demanded to know the dreams and visions of all his subjects, in order to obtain the explanation of the signs and prophecies that were tormenting and overwhelming him.

These wonders may simply demonstrate challenges to a still poorly consolidated authority, as well as the exasperation of populations subjugated by a tyrannical master.

The presence of Spaniards in parts of central America increases the anxiety provoked by gloomy prophecies

It is difficult to believe that the Spaniards passed completely unnoticed, having landed in 1492 in the West Indies, settled in Hispaniola and Cuba, and then established themselves on the coasts of Venezuela and Panama. For twenty years European fleets had been cruising between the islands and part of the continent and, when shipwrecks occurred, Indian canoes and Spanish ships spotted each other.

In 1517 a first Spanish expedition touched the coasts of Yucatán and the Campeche region. In May the following year a second expedition left Cuba, reached the island of Cozumel and moved up the Gulf of Mexico as far as Veracruz, before stopping at the mouth of the river Pánuco. There was trading, fighting and mutual observation.

The new arrivals were very strange, and the Indians wondered about the reason for this sudden invasion.... It was reported to Moctezuma that a mountain was moving around on the waters of the Gulf: a Spanish ship had been seen. The question was whether this was the prophesied return of the god Quetzalcoatl and his companions: Tula had collapsed with the departure of Quetzalcoatl, the Plumed Serpent, but the god-priest was to return in time from the distant east, in accordance with the pattern of cyclical repetition, and despite the new order of things. The conquering shadow of the Toltecs made its last appearance. Ironically, this image, which had never lost its power, loomed up again at the very time when the west was preparing to overwhelm the

Nezahualpilli spoke to Moctezuma in a dream as follows, showing him the future portents: 'I must inform you of strange and marvellous things which must come about during your reign.'

Diego Durán
The History of the Indies of New Spain, 1581

Signs of the divinatory calendar (below). Specialized priests, the *tonalpouhque*, interpreted the signs and numbers in circumstances like birth, marriage, the departure of merchants for far-off lands, the election of chiefs and in all exceptional situations.

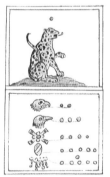

Aztecs. Thus history's trap was sprung: how could one try to retain a power inherited from Quetzalcoatl himself, if the god returned in person to reclaim it?

In 1519 an expedition leaves Cuba to explore the coasts of Mexico. At its head is a 33-year-old Spanish gentleman, Hernán Cortés

For several years already Moctezuma had been placing look-outs along the shores, to watch for the return of those who were perhaps gods guided by Quetzalcoatl. He knew that the Plumed Serpent would prove fatal to the worshippers of Huitzilopochtli. At all costs it was

Battle between Spaniards and Aztecs (left).

This headdress of green feathers (below) is mentioned in the long list of treasures that Cortés received from Moctezuma and sent to Charles V in July 1519; the latter gave it to his nephew as a gift.

vital to keep away the white men whose arrival from the eastern seas could only announce the return of the divine Plumed Serpent. Would not the best method be to make them offerings suited to the god whose emissaries they were?

When he learned in April 1519 that ships had berthed not far from what was to become the port of Veracruz, Moctezuma had the strangers' supplies replenished, and sent people to find out their intentions. He ordered that the visitors be offered jewels and feathers and, of course, human sacrifices.

Although disgusted by this offering, the Spaniards settled down some distance from the coast. Moctezuma then changed his

veyotlpan.   Conca qua mieqs mtlatoque
              q̃maca qyx q̃chqualom.

mind and mounted a first offensive against them,
dispatching his best sorcerers to bewitch the intruders.

**While the Spaniards continue their offensive,
Moctezuma continually hesitates about what to do**

In fact, the emperor did not really know whether he
should receive Cortés as a god or as his worst enemy.
Should he offer sumptuous hospitality and be as
conciliatory as possible, or should he try by all possible
means to turn the Spaniard's plans in a different
direction? Perhaps he was convinced from the
start that his end was unavoidable – this
theory would explain his continual
changes of mind, successively swinging
from resignation to indignation.
This conviction may also have
incited him gradually to abdicate
his powers, even before the
confrontation with the Spaniard.
For the present the Spaniards,
insensitive to native magic
because their flesh was 'hard', that
is impenetrable by evil spells, left
the torpor of the coastal region and
marched on Tenochtitlán. They had
decided to see things through to the end.
Having reached the highlands, they entered a
region dominated by Tlaxcala, and at first came up

"Doña Marina had
been a great lady and
a cacique [chief] over
towns and vassals since
her childhood. Her
father and mother were
lords of a town called
Paynala, which had
other towns subject
to it.**"**
Bernal Díaz del Castillo
*The Conquest of New
Spain*
Trans. J. M. Cohen
1963
Originally written
c. 1568

Here Marina stands
beside Cortés as
he receives gifts.

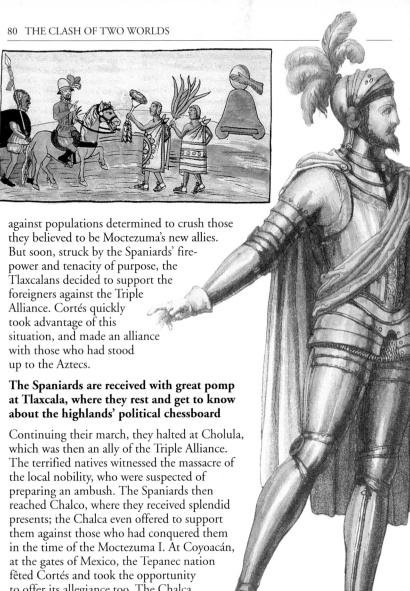

against populations determined to crush those they believed to be Moctezuma's new allies. But soon, struck by the Spaniards' fire-power and tenacity of purpose, the Tlaxcalans decided to support the foreigners against the Triple Alliance. Cortés quickly took advantage of this situation, and made an alliance with those who had stood up to the Aztecs.

The Spaniards are received with great pomp at Tlaxcala, where they rest and get to know about the highlands' political chessboard

Continuing their march, they halted at Cholula, which was then an ally of the Triple Alliance. The terrified natives witnessed the massacre of the local nobility, who were suspected of preparing an ambush. The Spaniards then reached Chalco, where they received splendid presents; the Chalca even offered to support them against those who had conquered them in the time of the Moctezuma I. At Coyoacán, at the gates of Mexico, the Tepanec nation fêted Cortés and took the opportunity to offer its allegiance too. The Chalca, Tepanecs, Tlaxcalans – all thirsting for revenge, all open breaches in the Triple Alliance's system.

On 8 November 1519 Cortés met the emperor Moctezuma at the entrance of Tenochtitlán: 'When we met I dismounted and stepped forward to embrace him, but the two lords who were with him stopped me with their hands so that I should not touch him.... When at last I came to speak with Moctezuma himself, I took off a necklace of pearls and cut glass that I was wearing and placed it round his neck ... a servant of his came with two necklaces, wrapped in a cloth, made from red snails' shells, which they hold in great esteem; and from each necklace hung eight shrimps of refined gold almost a span in length. When they had been brought he turned to me and placed them about my neck, and then continued up the street ... until we reached a very large and beautiful house which had been very well prepared to accommodate us.'

Hernán Cortés
Letters from Mexico
Trans. and ed. Anthony
R. Pagden, 1972
Originally written
1519–26

Left: a 19th-century version of the meeting. Opposite: Cortés meeting the Tlaxcalans.

The Spaniard's keen eye missed none of the signs that indicated the Aztecs' real weakness: the inferiority of their weapons, Moctezuma's hesitant attitude and the discontent of the subject peoples.

It was probably at this point that he perceived the possibility of forming an Indian confederation in his pay against the Triple Alliance. Any doubts that he might have had left him. Having founded the country's first Spanish town at Veracruz, he was given by the elected municipal council (in reality, his own army) all necessary administrative, judiciary and military powers for conquest and colonization, subject to Crown approval. His next move was to scuttle his ships, removing any temptation some of his men might have had to flee or seek new adventures, and settled in enemy territory.

"As the conversation went on ... we who were his friends advised him ... not to leave a single ship in port, but to destroy them all immediately, in order to leave no cause of trouble behind. For when we had marched inland others of our people might rebel like the last."

Bernal Díaz del Castillo
The Conquest of New Spain
Trans. J. M. Cohen
1963

Cortés is eager to meet the master of the Aztec world and discover the extent of his wealth and the reality of his powers

Cortés orders the ships to be destroyed (below).

At the same moment, Moctezuma, always prone to paralysing indecision, called together the rulers of Texcoco and Tacuba to organize the most sumptuous of receptions. All the great dignitaries and princes were invited to be present as the Spaniards arrived. The Spaniards were followed by native bearers bent double under the weight of the presents accumulated along the way.

This must have been an unforgettable spectacle: the meeting of two societies, two completely different cultures....

Moctezuma, the 'image of Huitzilopochtli', borne on his precious palanquin by lords, surrounded by his court and a multitude of slaves carrying offerings for the gods, went to meet Cortés.

The two processions came face to face. The sovereign placed a necklace of gold and precious stones around the Spaniard's neck, and gave him a splendid flower made of feathers.

Then they entered a nearby temple, where they received the homage of the rulers of Texcoco and Tacuba. The great dignitaries and lords came to worship Cortés, just as they did the god Huitzilopochtli. Moctezuma evoked the power that he derived from his 'father', the god Quetzalcoatl, whom he was ready to renounce; Cortés replied that he came in the name of a powerful lord, who reigned over a great part of the world, and of

Illustrations of Cortés at Moctezuma's court, painted in 1698.

"Moctezuma came to greet us and with him some two hundred lords, all barefoot and dressed in a different costume, but also very rich in their way and more so than the others."
Hernán Cortés
Letters from Mexico
Translated and edited by Anthony R. Pagden
1972

the one true God. From this meeting one can see that the Aztecs and the Spaniards were not playing the same game.

Whether by calculation or resignation, Moctezuma submits to his new masters. They immediately betray him

The procession set off to Tenochtitlán, where it was greeted by the priests to the sound of trumpets and conch-shells. Cortés and his people were lodged in the palace of Axayácatl, while the sovereign and other lords were immediately detained by the Spaniards and placed under a strong guard.

Worse was to follow: since the Aztecs still had superior forces, some Spaniards wanted to strike a great blow straight away. So, after receiving reinforcements, they

"Then he raised his clothes and showed me his body, saying, as he grasped his arms and trunk with his hands, 'See that I am of flesh and blood like you....' When he had gone we were well provided with chickens, bread, fruit and other requisites.... In this manner I spent six days...."

Hernán Cortés
Letters from Mexico
Translated and edited by
Anthony R. Pagden
1972

asked to be present at the ritual dances in celebration of the feast of Huitzilopochtli. This occasion provided them with an ideal opportunity to gather together and then massacre the most eminent members of the Aztec nobility. They are said to have killed almost 10,000 victims. Shortly afterwards, the rulers themselves were eliminated. Moctezuma was taken prisoner. Later he was mortally wounded by one of his own people (unless he was executed by the Spaniards – there is still some doubt). Cacamatzin, ruler of Texcoco, and the governor of Tlatelolco were strangled by the Spaniards.

Moctezuma, opposed to any uprising, sees his people's determination to confront the Spaniards

The surviving Aztec aristocrats did not throw in the towel, and were more determined than ever to finish off the invaders. After the brief reign of Cuitláhuac, the young Cuauhtémoc took over operations. The Aztecs surrounded the palaces where the Spaniards were living, with the firm intention of exterminating them. Once more, however, the Spaniards managed to save their skins.

On 30 June 1520, taking advantage of a moonless night and torrential rain, the Spaniards fled. Although they suffered extremely heavy losses, they reached the mainland. The Aztecs harried them, and thought themselves rid of these intruders for ever. It is said that Cortés wept at dawn when he realized the scale of the disaster of what was to be called the *Noche Triste*. But he was not a man to give up Tenochtitlán. Through Otumba, where he killed the head of the Aztec army with his own hand, he opened up the route to Tlaxcala. There he prepared a tremendous offensive against the Aztec capital, exploiting the dissensions that split the indigenous world. Cuauhtémoc failed to rally all the domains against the Spaniards. The Texcocans, the Chalca and the Tepanecs – all those which Tenochtitlán had previously subjugated or humiliated – took the side of the Spaniards.

At Texcoco, on the lake's eastern shore, one of Nezahualpilli's sons, Ixtlilxóchitl, put all his energy into supporting Cortés. The ruination of the Triple Alliance

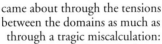

came about through the tensions between the domains as much as through a tragic miscalculation: the enemies of Tenochtitlán, especially the Tlaxcalans, believed that the Spaniards were going to help them eliminate the Aztecs.... They never suspected they were to be the next victims of a power whose resources and ambition they underestimated badly.

The siege of the capital Tenochtitlán will remain etched in the Aztec memory as a terrible nightmare

Cortés besieged the city for three whole months. He was able to count on the support

After the death of Moctezuma, while a prisoner of the Spaniards, his brother and cousin, Cuitláhuac and Cuauhtémoc respectively, became the leaders of the Aztecs. Cortés was besieged and resolved to leave the city. On a rainy night, the *Noche Triste*, the Spaniards succeeded in reaching one of the highways linking Tenochtitlán to the shore. But the Aztecs, once alerted, inflicted terrible losses: more than half the Spaniards and almost all their native auxiliaries were massacred or taken prisoner.

of several thousand natives, and constructed a flotilla of brigantines to secure control of the lake. Yet it took repeated attacks, famine and an epidemic brought by the Europeans to overcome the Aztecs' ferocious resistance.

The city finally fell on 13 August 1521. According to the chronicler Alva Ixtlilxóchitl, 'Almost all the Aztec

Cortés prepared his revenge for the *Noche Triste* by reconstituting his artillery and cavalry, and especially by building a small fleet of thirteen brigantines, thus overcoming his main military weakness: his inability to move around on water.

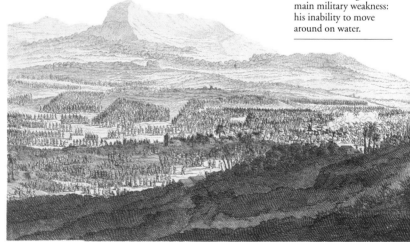

nobility died, the only survivors being a few lords and gentlemen, mostly children or extremely young people.' Cuauhtémoc, the 'last emperor', was taken prisoner and kept alive for a while, but then hanged on the pretext of a plot.

The Aztec empire had collapsed. Cortés set out to rebuild the capital and continue the conquest. A year later, in 1522, he became governor and captain-general of New Spain.

The apparatus of centralized domination built around the Triple Alliance is abruptly annihilated

The conquistador replaced the Triple Alliance with the distant authority of an unknown emperor who reigned beyond the ocean over Spain and part of Europe: Charles V. There were no longer any shifting coalitions, regularly questioning each other's supremacy. The Spaniards' weapons, tactics and energy were undoubtedly very important factors, but one should not overlook the fact that the conquistadors' victory was also won by a coalition of numerous states and peoples.

In July 1520, after the *Noche Triste* and Cortés' desperate flight from Tenochtitlán, an Aztec army tried, at Otumba, to cut short the retreat of Cortés and his Spaniards. After a tough battle the Spaniards, who suffered dramatic losses, finally emerged victorious and returned to Tlaxcala to recover their strength. There they dressed their wounds and prepared for the decisive assault on Tenochtitlán.

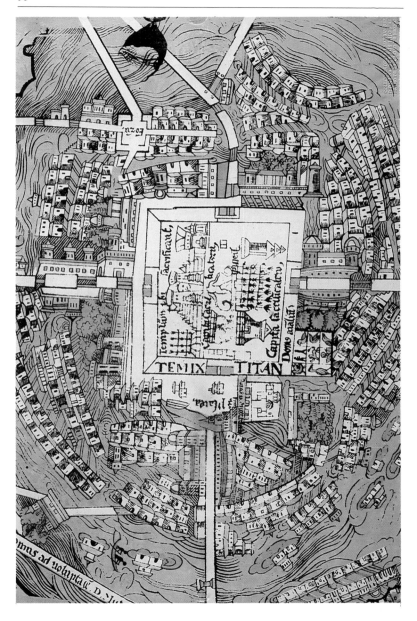

Those who had been the masters yesterday were not all resigned to defeat. Part of the Mexica and Texcocan aristocracy cherished the hope that the invaders would eventually leave. The 'anti-Spanish party' stubbornly believed in the restoration of the old order. Cortés set out to shatter these final illusions.

CHAPTER 5

FROM RESISTANCE TO COLLABORATION

Plan of the Aztec city of Tenochtitlán, made in the 16th century (opposite). Below: torture by savage dogs.

Cortés did not just impose submission to the Spanish Crown; he also demanded that the Indians convert to the Christian faith. He ordered an end to human sacrifices everywhere, and installed images of the new divinities in the native sanctuaries: the Virgin, Christ, the saints.... The Indians were astounded by the violence and passion with which the conquistadors broke the statues of their gods, whom they gave the defamatory name of idols. Cortés' conduct was inspired as much by gold and a love of power as by a desire to propagate the Christian faith – both because this faith justified his enterprise, and also because, in the spirit of the times, it could give it a goal and a meaning.

From 1525 onwards, with the arrival of a small but determined contingent of Franciscans, the pre-hispanic clergy was brutally forced to leave its sanctuaries and practice its rites in secret. The Spaniards carried out raids against the temples, assassinated pagan priests, set fire to the pyramids, smashed the statues and burned codices covered in pictographs. Iconoclastic violence replaced that of the sacrifices.

Idolatry – defined as everything that opposes the Christian faith – becomes the monster to be overthrown; and recalcitrant Indians are idolaters inspired by the devil

Nevertheless, the European monks succeeded in winning over part of the élite. But their success was both superficial and spectacular, as is shown by the hundreds of thousands of baptisms that the chroniclers of the time recorded imperturbably.

It is true that in these chaotic times, the years 1530–40, the monks introduced some semblance of order: around their churches and monasteries, under their often discretionary authority, life could reorganize itself. New rituals replaced the banned celebrations, new powers were substituted for those overthrown by the conquistadors.

The monks quickly became a force to be reckoned with, a force that could counterbalance the excesses of the Spanish soldiers and their native collaborators. This state of affairs was even more of blow for the 'idolaters'

"The idols are made of dough from all the seeds and vegetables which they eat, ground and mixed together, and bound with the blood of human hearts which those priests tear out while still beating ... after they are made they offer them more hearts."

Hernán Cortés
Letters from Mexico
Trans. and ed. A. R.
Pagden, 1972

At San Juan de Ulua, faced with the repeated refusal of the cacique to recant his beliefs, Cortés seized him, entered the temple, to the great alarm of the pagan priests and the people, and cast down the idols. The next day Father Bartolomeo de Olmedo, a monk of the Order of Mercy, celebrated the holy sacrament.

who saw their influence being undermined and their legitimacy called into question.

The arrival of Christianity shakes the native societies to their very foundations

The 'anti-Spanish party' rejected not only the new regime but also the new religious order, or rather the revolution brought about by Christianity, because its creed imposed a break with the past in condemning a great many of the principles by which the nobility had lived.

Thus, in the various sermons of the gospel-preachers, the ancestors of the Aztecs, the prestigious Toltecs, became monstrous idolaters condemned to burn for all eternity in the flames of hell. Christianity closed the schools where the nobility had always learned the ancient knowledge; it forbade human sacrifice, the consumption of the victims' flesh (that is, ritual cannibalism) and suppressed polygamy. Finally, it proscribed the taking of hallucinogenic plants. All these practices and privileges had always distinguished those in power from the common people, and maintained their legitimacy.

By imposing a uniform system of marriage, the Church destroys everywhere the traditional practice of alliances throughout the empire

Conversion, in particular, posed a threat to family cohesion – not only through the forced transition to monogamy, which threw thousands of secondary wives into the street together with their children (who henceforth became bastards without a name or a future), but also because the gospel-preachers did not hesitate to seize the children of the nobility to Christianize them and use them against their recalcitrant parents. The

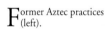

Former Aztec practices (left).

The archbishop of Mexico (above), Don Pedro Moya de Contreras, was the first of the inquisitors of New Spain.

A Dominican friar preaches to the Aztecs (opposite).

monks were well aware of the adults' resistance to them, so they chose to educate the young nobles in schools where they were taught the catechism, reading and writing. The children were thus converted, and so became their agents and spies.

Something else that scandalized the aristocracy was that the Christian religion claimed that all people were equal before God, and entrusted the powerful with the spiritual responsibility and the welfare of the humble. This attitude was truly unacceptable for a nobility that believed an impassable physical and spiritual barrier separated it from the common herd.

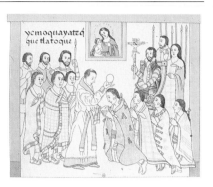

Convinced that Christianity means the overthrow of their system of values, the 'idolaters' try to resist the Spanish invader

But the attempts at conspiracy and at boycotting Spanish orders failed through lack of organization. Those who opposed Christianity were rapidly forced to become clandestine, and then to hand over their weapons. In any case, how could one live a clandestine life when power had always gone hand in hand with spectacular display?

The opposition disappeared little by little, through summary execution, accident or disease. One of the spokesmen in Texcoco was burned at the stake in 1539 for saying too loudly what many people were thinking at the time.

Other nobles, whether resigned to their fate, powerless, opportunistic or sincere, chose to collaborate. In this way they reckoned they might hold on to their most important powers, because they knew they possessed a precious trump card: their knowledge of men and terrain. Certainly the conquistadors had to rely on the native

The conversion of the Indians to Christianity was organized with brutal efficiency. Opposite: Spanish soldiers destroy Aztec idols. Above: baptism of the lords of Tlaxcala.

In 1539 the Inquisition struck a great blow by condemning Don Carlos Ometochtzin, the cacique of Texcoco, to the stake. Later a church was built there (below).

nobles taking over some roles if they wanted to extend their control over this immense territory, and also draw up an inventory of its resources and exploit them to their advantage.

One of the major obstacles confronting the Spaniards is the language barrier

Besides Nahuatl, over a hundred languages were spoken in New Spain. For the same reasons, the monks set out to Christianize the ruling class in the hope that its example would give a lead to the rest of the population. Members of the nobility did indeed prove to be the best allies of the gospel-preachers and their missionary aims.

In the first years collaboration with the victors paid off. The lords of Tlaxcala began this policy by being baptized, thus enabling them to retain relative autonomy until the end of the century. At Texcoco members of the ruling family also played the Spanish card; they made a decisive contribution in crushing the Mexica and helped the start of Franciscan evangelization.

The ambitions of yesteryear were henceforth reduced to very little: after having played the role of indispensable intermediaries between the invaders and the rest of the population, the great families gradually had to content themselves with the role of rich people of standing, with only local influence. As for Texcoco itself, it was eclipsed by the capital of New Spain, chosen by Cortés: Mexico City.

Women often play a crucial role in establishing Spanish domination

The daughters of the native aristocracy frequently became the concubines, and sometimes even the legitimate wives of the conquerors.

Moctezuma's daughter, Tecuichpotzin, is an excellent example of this. The wife of the last two Aztec monarchs, Cuitláhuac and Cuauhtémoc, in rapid succession, she was

It was Father Bartolomeo de Olmedo, who was entrusted by Cortés with baptizing the Indians. An intelligent man and an excellent theologian, he understood the Indians' temperament, and often intervened to moderate the conquistador's ardour and brutality.

baptized after the conquest, and given the name Isabella. Widowed by Cuauhtémoc at the age of sixteen, she still embodied a certain Aztec legitimacy, and constituted a figure of some importance on the new political chessboard. Cortés awarded her the revenues of the city

Raising the cross in an Aztec town.

of Tacuba in perpetuity, and then had her marry the conquistador Alonso de Grado. This Indian lady soon became a model of Hispanization and Christian piety. After Grado's death, she lived for a while in Cortés' 'harem', bore him a daughter, then remarried Spaniards on two occasions. Her last husband actively busied himself with increasing their fortune and pleading for her rights as Moctezuma II's heiress. She died in 1550, in total European luxury, after she had drawn up her will.

Her daughter Leonor was to marry the discoverer of the silver mines of Zacatecas, and some of her descendants would settle in Spain where they took the titles of the Count of Miravalle, Duke of Abrantés and of Linares.

Other families had less glittering but probably more representative destinies. For example, the mother and grandmother of Alva Ixtlilxóchitl, direct heirs of the rulers of Texcoco, married Spaniards who also undertook to defend their interests.

The marriages between native princesses and conquistadors, and the half-breeds who were the result, were undeniably to facilitate the transition between the two worlds.

The ruling class is renewed, and some people take the chance to denounce the old aristocracy

Minor provincial nobles and plebeians took advantage of the favour of the conquistadors and the Church to get involved in the circles of leadership. So they swelled the ranks of the collaborators, and the traditional nobility was reduced to sharing the title of cacique with these 'upstarts', as well as the role of governors given to them by the Spanish regime. Elected or nominated governors, these natives found themselves at the head of local populations grouped into communities, the *pueblos de indios*, which after 1530 were endowed with institutions transferred from the Iberian Peninsula.

However, the Spanish Crown was not always in favour

"The old cacique of Tlaxcala, Xicotenga, made this remark to Cortés: 'Malinche, to prove still more clearly how much we love you and wish to please you in all things, we want to give you our daughters for wives to bear you children.' **"**

Bernal Díaz del Castillo
The Conquest of New Spain
Trans. J. M. Cohen
1963

Lam. 2.

CORDILLERA
DE LOS
PUEBLOS,
QUE
ANTES DE LA CONQUISTA
PAGABAN TRIBUTO
A EL EMPERADOR
MUCTEZUMA,
Y
EN QUE ESPECIE,
Y
CANTIDAD.

The Spaniards had left Tabasco with twenty native women given to them by those they had conquered (opposite top). One of them, a young Aztec baptized Marina by the Spanish, became Cortés' mistress as well as his interpreter (opposite bottom).

of founding new élites. Towards the middle of the 16th century it even tried to reinstall the heirs of the former lords everywhere it seemed possible to do so, because it believed that the transference of power was compatible with respect for native hierarchies, providing that Spain's sovereignty was recognized.

From the very beginning the Crown sought to create and safeguard an 'Indian' identity, taking care to keep separate the indigenous and Spanish communities, or the two 'republics', to use the term of the period; the control of the former had to remain in the hands of the native nobility.

In this way they preserved the role of obligatory intermediary that was adopted by the legitimate or upstart caciques. It also meant that the term 'Indian' was established, henceforth designating all the natives, whatever their rank or their ethnic origin.

The fall of Mexico in no way tolls the knell of military campaigns for the Aztecs, who find employment in the service of the Crown

In the 1520s the pacifying of the centre of the country and the conquest of Guatemala and Honduras were carried out with the support of the valley's nobility and their troops. These same forces were to push back the attacks of the Chichimec Indians and guarantee access to northern Mexico's silver mines.

From 1541 to 1542 several tens of thousands of Mexica, Tlaxcalans and Otomís crushed the rebellion of Mixton, in the north-west part of the country, more than 600 km from Mexico. The bravest fighters among the Indians won military ranks there, together with coats of arms and titles, while throughout the 16th century their troops settled locally, in exchange for a few privileges.

luys pinello nahuathas

The Spanish colonization reversed the old pattern: henceforth it was to be 'civilized' Indians from the centre of the country who emigrated northwards to impose their sedentary ways on the nomads. Nothing could stop the retreat of the wild Indians, which continued its bloody progress until the 19th century.

From the 1540s onwards the new or traditional native ruling class promptly adapted to the world taking shape before its eyes. Not only did it very soon become familiarized with handling weapons and horses, but it learned accountancy, branched out into stockrearing or business, bought the goods being exported by Spain to its young colony, drank wine and wore silks.

It even acquired a sufficient mastery of Spanish legislation to make it work in its favour and defend its rights. This world of judges, governors, merchants and interpreters carved itself a place in colonial society, in the shadow of the conquerors but far above the indigenous masses.

The Church's education and the Indians' incredible ability to assimilate bear unexpected and remarkable fruit

One can speak of a true renaissance, in the sense that the meeting of cultures allowed a late flourishing in Mexico of the European renaissance. This renaissance found expression in the works of the native painters

The association of traditional pictographs with commentaries in Spanish shows how the two cultures came together at the time of the conquest: this account book (left) shows the officials involved and lists the types of services and objects supplied. Account books in codex form, like this one, were used very early on to record the economic, commercial and financial transformations introduced by the invaders.

Coat of arms of Spain (below) in the reign of Philip II (1556–98).

and sculptors who took part in building the churches, monasteries and chapels that now covered New Spain. Besides these masters of stone and the brush, who were in keeping with the best pre-hispanic tradition, there were also musicians and singers who proliferated in most settlements, learning the instruments of medieval Europe and, in some cases, tackling composition with a vigour that staggered the Spaniards.

But the most profound revolution was undoubtedly tied to the introduction of the European alphabet and, consequently, to the learning of writing. These Indians, whose culture had for centuries been based on pictographs and an oral tradition, learned to read and write under the monks' guidance.

A higher education was even provided for the most gifted among them within the college of Santa Cruz at Tlatelolco. They learned the language of Cicero, read the Latin classics and translated great European texts into Nahuatl. Some even familiarized themselves with typography and printing. Many became indispensable witnesses for the Franciscan and Dominican monks when they made their great ethnographic investigations into the pre-conquest societies. Others were to contribute to the knowledge of history.

The great 16th century chroniclers are a perfect illustration of the happy fusion of the two societies and the two cultures

The adoption of writing did not mean abandoning illustrated codices. Not only were the historians Chimalpahin, Ixtlilxóchitl or Tezozómoc still able to understand them, but well-read Indians learned to combine the pictographic tradition with European writing. They succeeded in making maximum use of these two modes of expression with an inventiveness and intelligence that display the astonishing fruitfulness of this period and of these well-to-do circles. But this admirable renaissance was to be smothered at birth by the colonial machine.

The indigenous painter Juan Gerson produced frescos of the *Apocalypse of Tecamachalco*. Like his contemporaries, he mixes indigenous and European elements in his compositions. The Indian painters succeeded in expressing colonial reality while meeting Spanish demands and remaining faithful to their art. It is probable that the systematic subjugation of the native elements to western iconographic conventions diverted them from their original meaning and usage. But out of this confrontation arose a unique artistic expression.

On the other hand, throughout the 16th century, the Indian masses were devastated by the shock of conquest: epidemics, ruthless exploitation and shattered values

Chaos took numerous forms. The ancestral guidelines that marked the differences between classes and origins foundered. The many signs of status disappeared – ostentatious clothing, participation in solemn celebrations, food privileges, which had reserved cacao, hallucinogens and the divine flesh of sacrificial victims for the nobles.

The power vacuum was also formidable: in 1521 the nobles and leaders tragically proved themselves powerless to oppose the foreigners. Even more serious was the death of the gods: from the end of the 1520s onwards, amid the general confusion and under pressure from the gospel-preachers, the sacrifices and cults that had always marked the cycles of time and ensured the working of the cosmos were interrupted, or definitively abandoned. So all the institutional frameworks that upheld the old societies were called into question or broken, with nothing to replace them in the first few decades, apart from the Christianity propagated by the Franciscans in a few cities.

Until the 1540s there was arbitrary rule. The conquistadors embarked greedily on a career of plunder, reduced the Indians to slavery, branded them with hot irons and worked them to exhaustion; while the extortions of the caciques often rivalled those of the Spaniards. Not content with eliminating the former priests and part of the nobility, the Spaniards reserved the priesthood for themselves and had a monopoly on the sacred, and hence on the meaning of existence.

However, it was especially by using

Codex with native pictographs and Spanish text, produced in 1554 under the instructions of a Spanish missionary. The gospel-preachers found pictures to be a handy means – especially at first – of overcoming their ignorance of the Indian languages.

a different language – it is extremely doubtful whether most Indians could catch its exact meaning – that Christianity and the Church destroyed not only the rules of the game but the game itself. There was total disarray, as can be seen in this testimony from one of the native Indians: 'The great freedom we now enjoy is pernicious because we are no longer forced to fear or respect anyone.'

When, in the mid-16th century, the Crown and the Church manage to impose some semblance of order, the people still have to try and survive the worst: epidemics

The scourge harvested its regular tribute of human lives. We do not know the precise nature of the illnesses that killed the Indians, commoners and nobles alike. Types of typhus and smallpox spread from the time of the siege of Tenochtitlán. Epidemics broke out in the whole country and raged almost continuously, with marked outbreaks in the years 1545–8, 1581–6 and 1629–31.

The lack of successful treatments, the moral and cultural distress, the human exhaustion, the absence of acquired immunity and of defence systems all explain the enormous mortality rate. Scared by the demographic fall, the Spaniards tried to understand the cause of this phenomenon that was depriving them of a precious labour force and a large amount of tribute. Seized with panic, the Indians attributed these catastrophes to the destruction of their way of life, the Spaniards' cruelty and the abandonment of the old gods who had stopped helping them. Most often they were simply dazed by their misfortune.

In the face of death's repeated assaults and the collapse of traditional institutions, many Indians quickly turned to alcohol, the pre-hispanic prohibitions having been swept aside with so many other things. Infanticides, abortions and suicides multiplied, an expression of the unbearable tragedy that these populations were experiencing on their own.

The break with former times merely began with the Spanish conquest. It would continue throughout the

All the medical knowledge of the Aztec doctors was helpless against the implacable plague of epidemics brought by the Spaniards (right). The illnesses were attributed to supernatural causes, to the will of gods, or the magic of sorcerers. The doctor (*ticitl*) resorted to divination, counter-magic or the laying-on of hands. In other cases he could be more effective: he knew how to reduce fractures, apply plasters, carry out bleedings, and above all prepare potions with medicinal plants.

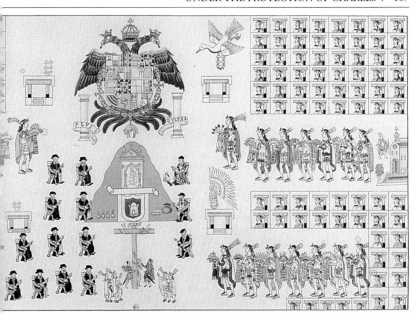

16th century and into the first decades of the 17th. There was no end to the death throes of a whole universe. It was left to the handful of survivors to reconstruct another world.

Painted at the request of the viceroy, Don Luis de Velasco, between 1550 and 1564, the *Codex Lienzo de Tlaxcala* is a work measuring 7m by 2.5m, which reconstructs the Tlaxcalan version of the conquest in the course of 87 tableaux. In the one above can be seen governors, viceroys and lords of Tlaxcala under the coat of arms of Charles V.

From the 17th century onwards, the native society disintegrated, shattered by the chaos that struck colonial Mexico. Even though some members of the nobility continued proudly to assert their pre-hispanic origins, their way of life was no longer anything but a replica, more or less faithful, of the Spanish model.

CHAPTER 6

THE AFTERMATH OF THE CONQUEST

Towards the end of the 16th century there were already more than 25,000 half-breeds in Mexico. Fifty years later there were 400,000. Their numbers grew rapidly because the Spanish emigrants were mostly male. Towards the end of the 18th century the number of half-breeds reached one and a half million. Opposite: a *lobo* (child of a mulatto and an Indian) with his Indian wife and their offspring. Left: Carmelita.

Without really disappearing, the native nobility was increasingly submerged, through the growing number of marriages with the Spaniards, in an intermediate half-breed world in which its identity was eventually dissolved.

At the turn of the 17th century a dilemma arises: how to retain one's indigenous identity while adapting to the Spanish model

This nobility now had to spare no effort in protecting the integrity of its patrimony and ensuring that the rank Spain had conceded to it was passed on, for imposters managed to infiltrate the caciques, despite lawsuits that sometimes dragged on for generations. Shaken by sordid quarrels, families of long standing sank into ruin, and with them the memory of ancient times became blurred. Nevertheless, in the mid-18th century there were still nobles powerful enough to constitute an important native pressure group in Mexico and Tlaxcala.

This group was closely tied to the Church and very proud of its blood and its origins; it continued to combine fortune, power and culture. Its spokesmen did not hesitate to visit Spain to plead the cause of the Mexican caciques and, if necessary, to demand loudly that the Indian population should be given the benefits of an education that would bring it out of the 'darkness of ignorance', 'because, when deprived of education, the natives' only rationale is what nature instils in them'.

At first the Spanish Crown watched the conquistadors from afar, leaving them more or less free to do as they chose. But then, mistrusting them, it determined that they should not enjoy the powers they were claiming for very long. In November 1529 the sovereign chose one of his civil-servants, a great lord, loyal, prudent and hardworking, to be his representative in Mexico with very extensive powers. Installed only in 1535, Antonio de Mendoza was the first – and also, from the start, one of the most remarkable – of the sixty-two viceroys who successively governed Mexico for almost three centuries. The era of conquistadors was followed by that of civil servants. Three great administrators, Antonio de Mendoza (1535–49), Luis de Velasco (1550–64) and Martín Enríquez (1568–80), gave Mexico a period of calm throughout the 16th century that enabled the conquest to continue and the country's economy to take a new course which was favourable to the victors' interests. Their palaces (right) dominated the towns and impressed the native lords (left).

Forma y Levantado de la

Por la correspondencia de los numeros se hallan en Est...

Nº 1. Conuentos de S. Fran.co   4 q. son S. Fran.co Tiago S. Diego S. Maria Ludonda.   Nº 7. Monxas.
Nº 2. De S.t Augustin   4 S.t Augustin S. Pable S. Ruastian S. Cruz
Nº 3. De S. Domingo.   2 que son S. Domingo y Porta Culi.   Nº 8. Hospitales
Nº 4. Padre de la Comp.a   4 Casa profesa los estudios S. Alfonso S. Anna nouiciado
Nº 5. Mercinarios   2 Nuestra S.a de la merced y Nra S.a de Belem.   Nº 9. Paroquias. 2.
Nº 6. Nra S.a del Carmen   1 Nra Senora de Montserrate   Nº 10. Colegios
Suma 18.   Suma 4.

A. Palacio Re.l
B. Cathedral.
C. Casa de Cabildo.
D. Casa Arp.l
F. Uniuersidad.
G. Alameda.
Las demas casas estan señaladas por
su distincion como se distinto partes
por la Pluma.

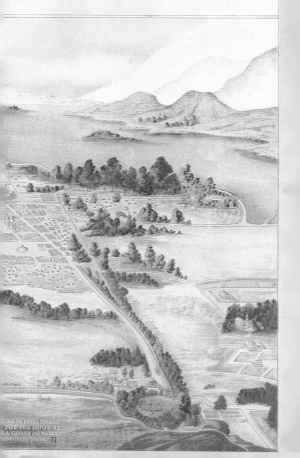

DAD DE MEXICO.
a Los conuentos y cosas señalados.

de Señora La Encarnacion S.ª Ynes S.ª Teresa. Ihs Maria la conception Son
descalsas S.ª Clara S.ª Isl. La penittencia. Regina coeli S.ª Monica la recoledas y S.ª Cruz Sama.ª
las Yndias de N.ª S.ª de Loreto de la pieta. S.ª de Juan de Dios de la misseri;
Ypolite y de San Lazaro
na. Martir, y la V.ª Cruz
S. Juan de Latran Colegio de Xpo. Colegio de las niñas.

DE S.ª J. MAX RAMIREZ
POR SUS HIJOS AL
LA CIUDAD DE MÉXICO
71

From pyramid to cathedral

Along the Zócalo in Mexico City (formerly the Plaza Mayor), the largest cathedral in Mexico displays its beautiful, mostly baroque façade of grey stone between two squat neo-classical towers. Begun in 1573, after the cabildo (municipal council) presented a request to Philip II, king of Spain, begging him to grant permission to erect a new cathedral worthy of the opulence of the New World, it was not until 1813 that it was completely finished. This cathedral replaced the excessively modest episcopal church built just after the conquest with materials taken from the pyramid of Huitzilopochtli, on a site located a little to the north-west of the present cathedral. The baroque part of the façade has three doors flanked by columns and surmounted by niches with carved ornamentation. All the differences of style in the cathedral bear witness to the fact that its construction was the work of several generations of architects.

This nobility learned the 16th-century gospel-preachers' lessons so well, along with the prejudices of the period, that it picked up the torch of Christianity, helped by those of its members who belonged to the Catholic clergy. While the nostalgic nobility tried to slow its decline, in the countryside native life was revived around the *pueblo* or ordinary people.

In 1531, at Tepeyac, the Virgin supposedly appeared several times to an Indian called Juan Diego. Since then many devoted people have come to the sanctuary of Our Lady of Guadalupe.

The colonial *pueblo* represents the village, the soil and the community

In the face of the splintering of the great pre-conquest ethnic and political groups, the collapse of memories and the epidemics, the Indians withdrew at the end of the 16th century to a community space around those who administered the village. From the mid-17th century onwards the aim of these minor dignitaries was to legitimize their power by forging themselves an identity and a place in colonial society and baroque Mexico. With this objective in mind they drew up and

The Indians continued to live in their traditional homes, cooking the food that they had always eaten. But some things changed: there is a painting of the Virgin on the wall, and the façade of the local church appears through the door.

passed on title deeds which placed on record the history of the *pueblo*.

Christianity appears as a crucial stage in the *pueblo*'s history

Far from being the exclusive prerogative of the nobles, alphabetic writing also helped people to set down community memories in the depths of the Aztec countryside. In these title deeds, the Christianization of the Indians, which had happened a century earlier, was no longer interpreted as a brutal coercion. The Church was now presented as the community's new axis, because it was the place where rituals occurred that once more punctuated its existence (baptisms, marriages and funerals). The choice of patron saint was seen, with the passing years, as a native initiative, and by the 17th century legends described how the saint revealed his desire to take the *pueblo* under his protection.

The *pueblo* authorities struggle desperately against those who try to reduce their rights and interfere with their lives

It was essentially the great Spanish landlords, the *hacendados*, and the parish priests who accorded the *pueblo*'s prerogatives the least recognition. The 17th and 18th centuries were filled with the echoes of the conflicts and lawsuits between Indians and *hacendados*. The heavy losses of human life caused by the epidemics left many uncultivated areas in which the Spaniards settled. But when, during the 18th century, the native population began growing again, and there was no longer enough land, disputes multiplied. From the second half of the 18th century onwards, tension increased and violent local revolts broke out.

Clashes with the priests were of a different kind, though they could be equally violent: in Indian eyes, it was a question of defending the status quo which allowed them to organize the community's religious life in their own way. Thus, whatever the adversary, it was within the framework of the *pueblo* that the natives applied themselves to preserving their patrimony of rights and beliefs, a colonial patrimony that in fact was an amalgamation of indigenous and European elements.

While the dignitaries forge a new community identity, the masses survive in a colonial society

For the people, there seemed to have been no changes in living and working conditions, tribute, food, language or everyday objects despite a century of Spanish

In the eyes of the Spanish colonists, the Indians represented first and foremost a workforce, indeed beasts of burden (below). Even before the end of the 16th century, Mexico's economic and social evolution began to transform the organization of native labour, with the rise and development of the great Spanish domains, the *haciendas*, which grew up outside the towns alongside the native *pueblos*. Opposite: *haciendas* and settlements of San Andrés Chalchicomula.

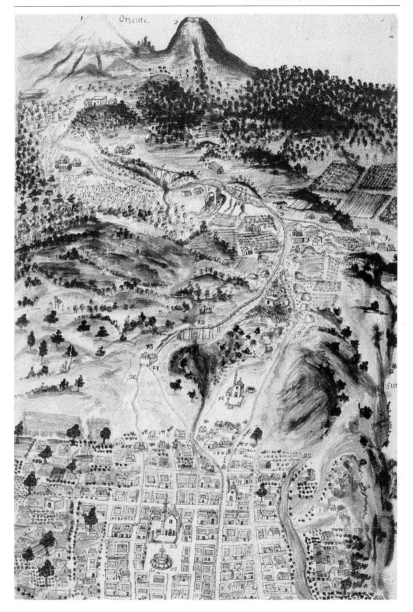

At Cuautitlán the crowds of Indians came from tens, even hundreds of kilometres around, on foot or donkey, to bring their vows and prayers, offer their gifts and fireworks, begging for help. The Virgin of Guadalupe remained the most venerated throughout Mexico. The processions were also the occasion for parading through the town with the baroque statues, which were often in painted wood and terrifyingly realistic, with a clear predilection for depicting bloody wounds and stigmata.

domination. The soil, the house and the maize fields kept their ancestral forces that people had been trying to placate from time immemorial. Yet by the first half of the 17th century, even before the end of the great epidemics, the survivors contrived to restore some meaning and balance to their existence by blending the cult of traditional powers – fire, water, the 'mountain inhabitants' or winds – with that of the saints who henceforth protected their village and home.

Little by little the Indians invented practices, beliefs and gestures of which there are still traces in the indigenous cultures today. The 17th century saw the flowering of a unique Christianity which allowed the Indians to express what remained of their original identity through an abundance of family devotions, the development of brotherhoods and the profusion of festivals. Calvary chapels, miraculous images, corridas, carnivals, processions and pilgrimages gave the Valleys of Mexico, Toluca or Puebla an ever-increasing resemblance to the Mediterranean countryside. Out of these colonized and colonial cultures there arose a reinvented Christianity.

From the 17th century onwards the Virgin of Guadalupe constitutes a widely popular cult

Contact with the half-breeds, mulattos and Spaniards who invaded the countryside caused this Christianity to undergo a further evolution in the 18th century. A common culture now took shape which mixed all kinds of beliefs and practices, foreshadowing the popular cultures of modern Mexico, in which the indigenous heritage gradually dissolved.

Yet it was in the towns that true change occurred, especially in the capital of New Spain. Here, from the 16th century onwards, the Indians became familiar with the Spanish tongue and also underwent the experience of all kinds of biological, social and cultural interbreeding.

They learned to move between two worlds, that of the Spanish masters in whose service they obtained posts, and that of a community where the constraints sometimes became unbearable.

Many of them were bilingual, *ladinos* or *españolados* (that is, Hispanicized), to use the contemporary terms, and knew how to use their origins to advantage, or to benefit from assimilation and anonymity. By the 17th century neither their

In each parish, the priest generally had three sacramental registers: one for the whites, another for the Indians, and the third for those of mixed blood. More or less official classifications had been established that distinguished up to sixteen categories of mixed blood depending on the respective proportions of European, Indian or black blood. Legally superior to the half-breeds, the Indians often held a lower social position when the half-breed (foreman, employee or servant) was invested with his master's authority. Later, the terms Indian and half-breed began to designate social categories rather than notions, which did not prevent marriages uniting couples belonging to two different ethnic groups (left).

clothing nor their haircuts seemed to give them any distinction from the Spanish population any longer.

Like a magnet the city attracted the Indians from the villages, either because they were over-exploited or because they had resolved to break their community ties. This was a fascination that dated back a long time when one recalls the nomads who prowled around the Toltec cities centuries before, in order to glean some fragments of civilization.

The West sets its traps: the hope of easy gains and pleasures, the lure of alcohol, the illusion of escaping one's ethnic origins

In cities the Indians very soon assimilated the negative aspects of 'culture' brought by the Spaniards. The most spectacular expression was drunkenness or, rather, alcoholism which struck a great part of the indigenous population.

The public houses or *pulquerías* were the setting for shoddy scenes: it was here that husbands squandered the meagre household income, women passed out and miscarried, bloody brawls broke out and sordid prostitution was carried on. In 1784 the capital had more than 600 *pulquerías*, each of which could easily contain a hundred customers inside or nearby. It is also true to say that it was in the *pulquerías*, away from the parish and community, that the Indians learned about half-breed society, and co-existence and complicity with blacks, mulattos and all those of mixed blood. Although the taverns housed the depths of delinquency, corruption and clandestine love affairs,

In the 17th century and even at the beginning of the 18th the preparation of pulque was still accompanied by ritual practices and burnt offerings, and the drinking sessions that punctuated the brotherhood festivals, funerals and Christian solemnities, even in the great cities, all echo the collective ceremonies before the conquest. But by the late 18th and 19th centuries the *pulquerías* showed the influence of the conquerors (opposite above).

By 1750 no less than 10,000 Indians had migrated to the towns, employed ever since in all the subordinate jobs, all the little trades: as porters, bearers, water-sellers, tortilla-vendors, servants in the rich houses of half-breeds (opposite below), or as sellers of chickens (left).

they were also places for living life to the full and for relaxing. These *pulquerías* were alternatives to a rigid society that sought to assign everyone a fixed place depending on their race and wealth, and in many ways were the crucible from which the popular cultures and the 'poverty cultures' of modern Mexico were to arise.

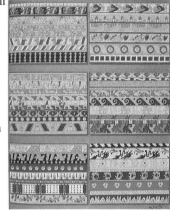

By the second half of the 16th century, a reduced, uprooted and mobile population was discovering in the silver mines the pressures of salaried work in more or less permanent and specialized teams.

In one generation these workers went through stages of acculturation that it took others several centuries to achieve.

Like the mines, forced labour in those prison-like workshops known as *obrajes* wore people out in body and soul by tearing them away from their family circle and delivering them to an unfamiliar, frenzied and dead-end way of life. For other Indians, however, craftsmanship, selling foodstuffs, and employment as servants offered less painful avenues that allowed them to melt into the half-breed world and escape destitution.

From the end of the 18th century the Indians who survived the epidemics, interbreeding and colonial exploitation face the first onslaughts of the modern world

Paradoxically it was the ideals of the Enlightenment and Independence that again brought into the question the Indian way of life, abruptly upsetting the balance that the indigenous communities had recovered with such difficulty. Henceforth anxious to civilize (and no longer to Christianize, as in the 16th century), the state intervened and imposed schoolmasters everywhere, together with the teaching of the Spanish tongue. In the same period, around 1780, it was preoccupied with economies, and set out to abolish or severely restrict the most spectacular features of indigenous culture: religious theatre, brotherhoods, processions and festivals. The Crown was of the same mind, and was soon to revise its policy towards the

A crucial institution of ancient Mexican societies, the tradition of the almost daily market lasted through the centuries. This institution conserved all its vigour and, with colonization, took on an extra meaning: the market was no longer just the place for doing deals around sellable commodities like the highly individual textile (opposite above), it was also the place for exchange and meetings, the mixing of social classes and of races. The marketplace was where, for a while, half-breeds, Indians and whites occupied the same ground and spoke a common language (left).

communities: in the 19th century it abolished all legal difference between Indians and Spaniards. Should one hail the paternalism of an 'enlightened' power that wanted to educate these Indians and improve their material existence, or see in this the first striking of blows against cultures which had barely assimilated the heritage of the century of conquest and of the baroque 17th century?

When it became independent in 1821, the young Mexico, out of concern for democracy and equality, confirmed these measures. It turned the Indians into citizens like any others, and set out to privatize – that is, to sell to individuals – the communal lands from which the *pueblo* derived a good deal of its resources. This was a death sentence on the indigenous communities.

In Mexico the indigenous districts, distant heirs of pre-hispanic Tenochtitlán and Tlatelolco, disappeared, absorbed by the modern city. Afterwards the Indians could only stand aside to make way for the speculators and lose themselves in the mass of the half-breed population. Still more wrongs were to undermine the rural communities throughout the 19th century: the extension of the great landed property, the *hacienda*, was to turn the native peasants into agricultural workers who were in debt for life, tied to their master's land and subject to his all-powerful despotism. Although the revolution of 1910 put an end to this new servitude, it could not slow down the irreversible destruction of the edifice that the Indians had rebuilt so laboriously under Spanish domination.

Are the heirs of the Aztecs today no more than images for art books, silhouettes in comic strips or characters in revolutionary epics?

Some villages, some enclaves resisted modernization longer than others, but the 1940s, with the abrupt rise of industrialization, opened up the era of massive migrations to the cities and the final abandonment of a soil that had become incapable of feeding numerous families. In the Valley of Mexico the fauna and flora of a thousand years, and the ancestral landscape, were engulfed by the megalopolis. Is all we have left of the

" Mexico today still carries the stamp of its Indian origin, the mark of those Aztecs whose language impregnates spoken Spanish, and who left enough traces of their intellectual and artistic capacities to make one look on the future of that country with confidence.**"**
Jacques Soustelle
The Four Suns, 1957

Aztecs descendants a mute craftsmanship, a mixture of the heritage of distant pre-hispanic times, the Spanish colony and the 19th century?

And yet the Indians still exist. But they scarcely have the means any longer of escaping the anonymity of an industrial society that makes the mirages of the consumer age shimmer at the very doors of their shanty towns. A thousand years after the Toltecs and Tula, five hundred years after the Mexica and Tenochtitlán, the city of the end of our own century, with its twenty million inhabitants, has in its turn closed its doors on bewitched and defeated emigrants....

Tampico, today one of Mexico's leading ports, lies about six miles up the Pánuco river on the Gulf of Mexico. In 1836 (below) it was already an important town, though low-lying and subject to flooding.

Tunas

DOCUMENTS

Myths, narratives, historical
reconstructions: a destiny that can
be read like an open book.
A flamboyant people
who passed abruptly from history
into legend.

The origins of the world and of men

In the beginning darkness ruled. The gods assembled before the light. The humblest of them fell into it: he became the sun.... Thus began Aztec cosmogony.

The five suns

The Aztec myth of the five suns explains man's destiny and his unavoidable end....

Here is the oral account of what is known of how the earth was founded long ago.
One by one, here are its various foundations [ages].
How it began, how the first Sun had its beginning 2513 years ago – thus it is known today, the 22 of May, 1558.

Solar year of eighteen months of twenty days, plus five days of evil omen.

Codex of the sun depicting the cult of Tonatiuh.

This Sun, 4-Tiger, lasted 676 years. Those who lived in this first Sun were eaten by ocelots. It was the time of the Sun 4-Tiger.

And what they used to eat was our nourishment, and they lived 676 years. And they were eaten in the year 13. Thus they perished and all ended. At this time the Sun was destroyed. It was in the year 1-Reed. They began to be devoured on a day [called] 4-Tiger. And so with this everything ended and all of them perished.

This Sun is known as 4-Wind. Those who lived under this second Sun were carried away by the wind. It was under the Sun 4-Wind that they all disappeared.

They were carried away by the wind. They became monkeys.

Their homes, their trees – everything was taken away by the wind.

And this Sun itself was also swept away by the wind.

And what they used to eat was our nourishment.

[The date was] 12-Serpent. They lived [under this Sun] 364 years. Thus they perished. In a single day they were carried off by the wind. They perished on a day 4-Wind. The year [of this Sun] was 1-Flint.

This Sun, 4-Rain, was the third. Those who lived under this third Sun, 4-Rain, also perished. It rained fire upon them. They became turkeys. This Sun was consumed by fire. All their homes burned.

They lived under this Sun 312 years. They perished when it rained fire for a whole day.

And what they used to eat was our nourishment.

[The date was] 7-Flint. The year was 1-Flint and the day 4-Rain.

They who perished were those who had become turkeys.

The offspring of turkeys are now called

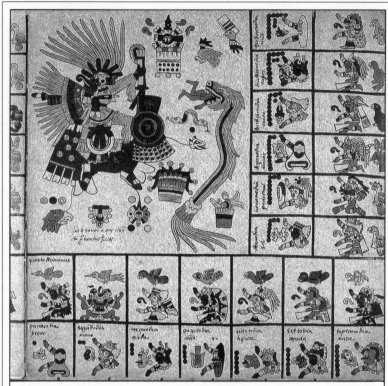

A month of the *Codex Borbonicus*, with the god Xipe Totec.

pípil-pípil.

This Sun is called 4-Water; for 52 years the water lasted.

And those who lived under this fourth Sun, they existed in the time of the Sun 4-Water.

It lasted 676 years.

Thus they perished: they were swallowed by the waters and they became fish.

The heavens collapsed upon them and in a single day they perished.

And what they used to eat was our nourishment.

[The date was] 4-Flower. The year was 1-House and the day 4-Water. They perished, all the mountains perished.

The water lasted 52 years and with this ended their years.

This Sun, called 4-Movement, this is our Sun, the one in which we now live.

And here is its sign, how the Sun fell into the fire, into the divine hearth, there at Teotihuacán.

It was also the Sun of our Lord Quetzalcoatl in Tula.

The fifth Sun, its sign 4-Movement,

is called the Sun of Movement because it moves and follows its path.
And as the elders continue to say, under this Sun there will be earthquakes and hunger, and then our end shall come.

Quoted in Miguel León-Portilla
Aztec Thought and Culture
Translated by Jack Emory Davis, 1963
Copyright © 1963 by the University of Oklahoma Press, Norman, Oklahoma

The Aztec calendar stipulates that the world collapsed four times. The present world, the fifth, that of the sun of movement, was born on 4-Ollin.

In the traditions and chronicles written up after the conquest as well as in pre-Columbian manuscripts and in the bas-reliefs of some monuments, one encounters the idea that our world was preceded by four worlds or 'suns' which ended in cataclysms. These vanished worlds are called the 'Tiger Sun' (*Ocelotonatiuh*), 'Wind Sun' (*Eecatonatiuh*), 'Rain Sun' (*Quiauhtonatiuh*) and 'Water Sun' (*Atonatiuh*). The Rain Sun is also sometimes known as the 'Fire Sun' (*Tletonatiuh*), because it was a rain of fire that destroyed the world at the end of this period.

These four ages are not always described in the same order of succession. According to the *Anales de Cuauhtitlán*, the first of the suns was the Water Sun, followed by those of the Tiger, Rain and Wind. The *Historia de los Mexicanos por sus pinturas* gives the following order: Tiger, Wind, Rain, Water, which is corroborated by the magnificent monument known as the 'Aztec Calendar'. This famous bas-relief, like those of the 'stone of the suns',

The fire relit in the temple.

enumerates the four ages in the same order as the *Historia*, each age being represented by a date, that of the cataclysm that ended it. These dates are:
4-*Ocelotl* (4-Tiger), end of the Tiger Sun.
4-*Eecatl* (4-Wind), end of the Wind Sun.
4-*Quiauitl* (4-Rain), end of the Rain Sun.
4-*Atl* (4-Water), end of the Water Sun.

Finally, our present world is marked on the 'Aztec Calendar' by the date of 4-*Ollin* (4-movement, or earthquake), when our sun began moving, four days after its birth. In the ritual calendar, this is the festival of the sun and of the lords. But it is also probably the date when our world will end in earthquakes, the sign *ollin* symbolizing both the sun's movement and seismic shocks.

In the *tonalamatl*, or divinatory calendar, all days bearing the number 4 are considered an ill omen. The day of 4-*Ocelotl*, end of the Tiger Sun, is a day of ill omen, dominated by the god Tezcatlipoca. Tezcatlipoca, god of the north, of cold and of night, turned himself into a tiger, according to the *Historia de los Mexicanos*, to throw down the sun. The first age, according to the

Anales de Cuauhtitlán, ended in cold and darkness, following an eclipse.

The date 4-*Eecatl*, end of the Wind Sun, is considered a day of enchantments and sorcery. The day 1-*Eecatl* is the day of the sorcerer *par excellence*. In fact, it was by a vast magic operation that the second world ended: all men were turned into monkeys. At the same time a violent wind was blowing, the manifestation of *Eecatl*, god of the wind, who is one of the forms of Quetzalcoatl. The idea that the men of one of the vanished worlds were changed into monkeys is also found in the great Quiché Maya chronicle, the *Popol-Vuh*. Among Central Mexicans, this idea was linked to the actions of the god Quetzalcoatl in the form of the wind divinity, protector of magicians.

The date 4-*Quiauitl*, end of the Rain Sun, is placed under the protection of Tlaloc, god of rain, and it is this god's mask, recognizable by its long teeth and enormous eyes, that is used as the sign of rain. The third world collapsed under a rain of fire. Tlaloc was not only god of rain, although this was his most usual function, but also god of fire that falls from the sky – lightning and thunder, and perhaps volcanic eruptions; this is the rain of fire (*tlequiauitl*).

The date 4-*Atl*, end of the Water Sun, is represented on the monuments mentioned above by the number 4 accompanied by the face of the goddess Chalchiuhtlicue, 'she who wears a skirt of precious stone', a water divinity and companion of Tlaloc; she seems to emerge from a receptacle. Here, one is clearly dealing with water, because the fourth world ended in inundations, in a kind of flood.

Thus, on four occasions, a world was born and collapsed in gigantic

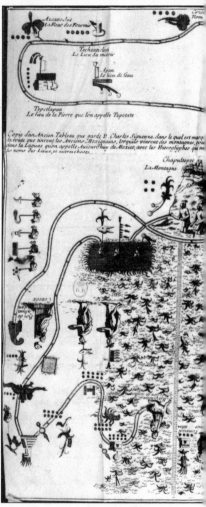

The long migration of the ancient Mexicans to Tenochtitlán.

catastrophes. Today's world will suffer the same fate. The ancient Mexicans conceived this history of the universe as that of victories and defeats of the alternating principles, taking turns to rule over everything, then driven away and deprived of any grip on the real world. The first of the suns is that of Tezcatlipoca; this is the age of cold, the night, the north. The second, under the influence of Quetzalcoatl, god of the west, is the period of sorcery and of the west. The third is dominated by Tlaloc who, as god of rain, is a divinity of the south. The fourth, sun of water and of

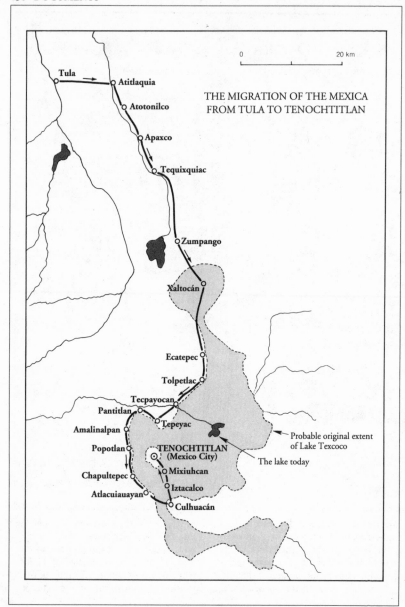

THE MIGRATION OF THE MEXICA
FROM TULA TO TENOCHTITLAN

0   20 km

Tula

Atitlaquia

Atotonilco

Apaxco

Tequixquiac

Zumpango

Xaltocán

Ecatepec

Tolpetlac

Tecpayocan

Pantitlan

Tepeyac

Amalinalpan

Popotlan

TENOCHTITLAN
(Mexico City)

Chapultepec

Mixiuhcan

Iztacalco

Atlacuiauayan

Culhuacán

Probable original extent
of Lake Texcoco

The lake today

Chalchiuhtlicue, is a period of the east, because water and its goddess belong to the east. As for today's sun, the fifth, it is the sun of the centre because five is the number of centre; the divinity of the centre is Xiuhtecutli, god of fire: hence our sun is a fire-sun, sometimes represented by the same symbol as fire, a butterfly....

The tradition concerning the four suns is just one example of the way people think in every area: the interpretation of all the phenomena in the world through the alternation of fundamental aspects of reality which follow and replace each other, triumph and disappear, and which are linked to the directions of space.

The cosmogonic myths contain few indications as to the way they envisaged the world's inhabitants in these vanished epochs. There was generally a belief that there were giants in those days, then men who lived on wild grasses. The ancient Mexicans had a very clear sense of the superiority of their agricultural civilization over that of the nomadic tribes, the Chichimecs, who wandered in the semi-desert region of the north. They themselves, before reaching the central plateau, had led this precarious way of life in the cactus steppes. As opposed to the civilization of maize, of which they were the trustees, they depicted their ancestors of the dead suns as barbarians who were ignorant of agriculture – which they too, in fact, had been until only a few centuries earlier.

Between the end of the fourth sun and the start of ours, they placed a transitional period, supposed to have lasted twice-times-thirteen years: the years, in the count of time, are divided into series of thirteen, each of these series being attached to one of the cardinal points: in four '13s', a native 'century', the 52-year cycle, was completed.

The 'fall of the sky', no doubt the deluge that put an end to the Water Sun, took place in the year 1-*Tochtli* (1-Rabbit), the year of the south. The gods Quetzalcoatl and Tezcatlipoca undertook the raising of the sky; and when the task was completed, Tezcatlipoca changed his name, becoming Mixcoatl, god of the north, in the year 2-*Acatl* (2-Reed): in the divinatory calendar, the day 2-*Acatl* was devoted to Tezcatlipoca. During the eighth year the *macehualtin* were created, the working men. Men were needed for the future sun, men destined to be sacrificed and to nourish the heavenly body with their blood.

With the second 'thirteen' of years, which starts with the year 1-*Acatl*, one enters the domain of the east. *Ce acatl* (1-*Acatl*-Reed) is the cyclic name of Quetzalcoatl, as god of the east and of the morning star, of resurrection. All of the fifth sun will be dominated by this great theme of death and rebirth, of the sacrifice necessary to the life of the heavenly bodies and of the universe. In the year 1-*Acatl*, the gods decide to create the sun. But for that it is already necessary to spill blood, liberate the life forces; and one can only liberate them by killing, by sacrifice and by war. The gods unleash war, taking part themselves on occasions. The last year of the second series, 13-*Acatl*, is that of the sun's birth.

Jacques Soustelle
The Universe of the Aztecs, 1979

The creation of man

After the gods had assembled at Teotihuacán and the sun had been created, they asked themselves who would inhabit the earth....

And then Quetzalcoatl went to *Mictlan*. He approached Mictlantecuhtli and Mictlancíhuatl [Lord and Lady of the region of the dead]; at once he spoke to them:

'I come in search of the precious bones in your possession. I have come for them.'

And Mictlantecuhtli asked of him, 'What shall you do with them, Quetzalcoatl?'

And once again Quetzalcoatl said, 'The gods are anxious that someone should inhabit the earth.'

And Mictlantecuhtli replied, 'Very well, sound my shell horn and go around my circular realm four times.'

But his shell horn had no holes. Quetzalcoatl therefore called the worms, who made the holes. And then the bees went inside the horn and it sounded.

Upon hearing it sound, Mictlantecuhtli said anew, 'Very well, take them.'

But Mictlantecuhtli said to those in his service, 'People of *Mictlan*! Gods, tell Quetzalcoatl that he must leave the bones.'

Quetzalcoatl replied, 'Indeed not; I shall take possession of them once and for all.'

And he said to his *nahualli* [double], 'Go and tell them that I shall leave them.'

And the *nahualli* said in a loud voice, 'I shall leave them.'

But then he went and took the precious bones. Next to the bones of man were the bones of woman;

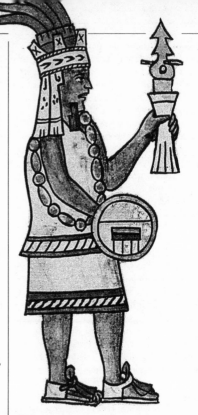

T zapotla Tena, one of the Aztec gods.

Quetzalcoatl took them....

And again Mictlantecuhtli said to those in his service, 'Gods, is Quetzalcoatl really carrying away the precious bones? Gods, go and make a pit.'

The pit having been made, Quetzalcoatl fell in it; he stumbled and was frightened by the quail. He fell dead and the precious bones were scattered. The quail chewed and gnawed on them.

Then Quetzalcoatl came back to life; he was grieved and he asked of his *nahualli,* 'What shall I do now...?'

And the *nahualli* answered, 'Since things have turned out badly, let them turn out as they may.'

And he gathered them ... and then he took them to *Tamoanchan.*

And as soon as he arrived, the woman called Quilaztli, who is Cihuacóatl, took them to grind and put them in a precious vessel of clay.

Upon them Quetzalcoatl bled his member. The other gods and Quetzalcoatl himself did penance.

And they said, 'People have been born, oh gods, the *macehuales* [those given life or "deserved" into life through penance].'

Because, for our sake, the gods did penance!

Mexican manuscript of 1558
Quoted in Miguel León-Portilla
Aztec Thought and Culture
Translated by Jack Emory Davis, 1963

The duties of man

Speeches, poems and precepts reveal the Indians' conception of existence and the duties of everyone on earth. They exalt the value of work, respect and obedience, recommending just measures and self-control.

Act! Cut wood, work the land,
plant cactus, sow maguey;
you shall have drink, food, clothing.

With this you will stand straight.
With this you shall live.
For this you shall be spoken of, praised;
in this manner you will show yourself
  to your parents and relatives.

Someday you shall tie yourself to a skirt
  and blouse.
What will she drink? What will she eat?

The maguey (agave) from which the Indians extracted sap to obtain pulque.

Is she going to live off the air?
You are the support, the remedy;
you are the eagle, the tiger.

Receive this word, listen to this word.
I hope that for a little time you will live
  with Our Lord,
He who is Master of the Close Vicinity.
Live on earth;
I hope you will last for a little time.
Do you know much?
With good judgment, look at things,
  observe them wisely.
It is said that this is a place of hardship,
of filth, of troubles.
It is a place without pleasure, dreadful,
  which brings desolation.

There is nothing true here....
Here is how you must work and act;
safely kept, in a locked place,
the elders left us these words
at the time of their departure.

Those of the white hair and the
   wrinkled faces,
our ancestors....

They did not come here to be arrogant;
they were not seeking;
they were not greedy.
They were such
that they were highly esteemed on earth;
they came to be eagles and tigers.

Do not throw yourself upon women
like the dog which throws itself upon
   food.
Be not like the dog
when he is given food or drink,
giving yourself up to women before
   the time comes.

Even though you may long for women,
hold back, hold back with your heart
until you are a grown man, strong and
   robust.
Look at the maguey plant.
If it is opened before it has grown
and its liquid is taken out,
it has no substance.
It does not produce liquid; it is useless.
Before it is opened
to withdraw its water,
it should be allowed to grow and attain
   full size.
Then its sweet water is removed
all in good time.

This is how you must act:
before you know woman
you must grow and be a complete man.
And then you will be ready for marriage;
you will beget children of good stature,
healthy, agile, and comely....

At dawn the judges would be seated on
their mats, and soon people would begin
to arrive with their quarrels. Somewhat
early, food would be brought from the
palace. After eating the judges would

Education of children and adolescents from the *Codex Mendoza*.

rest a while, and then they would
continue to listen until two hours before
the sun set. In matters of appeal there
were twelve judges who had jurisdiction
over all the others, and they used to
sentence with the sanction of the ruler.

Every twelve days the ruler would
meet with all of the judges to consider
all of the difficult cases.... Everything
that was taken before him was to have
been already carefully examined and
discussed. The people who testified
would tell the truth because of an oath
which they took, but also because of the
fear of the judges, who were very skilled
at arguing and had a great sagacity for
examination and cross-examination.
And they would punish rigorously those
who did not tell the truth.

The judges received no gifts in large
or small quantities. They made no
distinction between people, important

Tlaloc, messenger of Huitzilopochtli.

or common, rich or poor, and in their judgments they exercised the utmost honesty with all. And the same was true of the other administrators of the law.

If it were found that one of them had accepted a gift or misbehaved because of drinking, or if it were felt that he was negligent ... the other judges themselves would reprehend him harshly. And if he did not correct his ways, after the third time they would have his head shorn. And with great publicity and shame for him they would remove him from office. This was to them a great disgrace.... And because one judge showed favouritism in a dispute towards an important Indian against a common man and gave a false account to the lord of Tezcoco, it was ordered that he be strangled and that the trial begin anew. And thus it was done, and the verdict was in favour of the common man.

Indian poems by Andrés de Olmos and narrative by Alonso de Zurita, Bernardino de Sahagún's informant Quoted in Miguel León-Portilla *Aztec Thought and Culture* Translated by Jack Emory Davis, 1963

The myth of Quetzalcoatl

Quetzalcoatl was held in high esteem and considered to be god; he was worshipped at Tula from the remotest time. His very high temple had been a staircase with steps so narrow that a foot could not get a firm hold. His statue was always in a recumbent position and covered with *mantas* [tapestries]. His face was very ugly, bearded, with an elongated head. His servants or subjects were all workers in the mechanical arts, and very skilled at working the green stone called *chalchiuitl*, melting silver, and many other crafts of this kind.

All these trades had their source and origin in Quetzalcoatl, who possessed houses made of the precious stone called *chalchiuitl*, or constructed of silver, red and white mother-of-pearl, boards, turquoise and rich featherwork. His subjects were very quick to reach any place wherever it was. There is a hill called Tzatzitepetl (it is still called this today) where there lived a public crier whose job it was to make announcements. He could be heard in the towns and villages even a hundred leagues away in the Anahuac. They heard his voice over these long distances, and immediately hurried to see what Quetzalcoatl desired.

It is also said that this god was very rich, and that he had all manner of food and drink; his maize was very abundant, his calabashs as big around as an armspan; his maize cobs were so long

Quetzalcoatl

that their length was measured in armspans; the white-beet stalks too were very long, and so big you could climb them like a tree. All colours of cotton were sown and gathered – red, scarlet, yellow, brown, whitish, green, blue, black, dark, orange and buff, with the peculiarity that these colours were natural and originated from the plant.

It is also said that in the above-mentioned town of Tula, many types of richly feathered birds were bred, in a great variety of colours, which are called *xiuhtototl, quetzaltototl, çaquan* and *thauhquechol,* and many others besides which had the sweetest of songs.

Quetzalcoatl, moreover, possessed all the riches of the world, in gold and silver, in green stones called *chalchiuitl,* and in other precious things, as well as a great abundance of cacao trees of different colours. Quetzalcoatl's vassals were very rich and wanted for nothing; there was no shortage of food, no lack of maize. They had no need at all to feed on little cobs, which they used only as

fuel for burning, to heat their baths.

It is also said that Quetzalcoatl underwent penance by pricking his legs and withdrawing blood with which he coated thorns of maguey. He washed at midnight in a fountain called *xicapoyan,* and it was from this that the priests and ministers of the Mexican idols later adopted Quetzalcoatl's custom in the town of Tula.

Time put an end to the fortune of Quetzalcoatl and the Toltecs; because three sorcerers came against them, called Uitzilopochtli, Titlacauan and Tlacauepan, who carried out a great number of tricks in the town of Tula.

It was Titlacauan who began, in the disguise of a white-haired old man. In this form he went to Quetzalcoatl's palace where he said to his pages: 'I want to see the king and speak to him.' 'Get out!' was the reply. 'Clear off, old man, you can't see him; he's ill; you would just annoy him and disturb him.' So the old man said: 'I must see him.' The pages replied: 'Wait.'

So they went to tell Quetzalcoatl that an old man wanted to speak to him, and they added: 'Lord, we showed him the door so he would go away, but he refuses to go, and says he absolutely must see you.' Quetzalcoatl replied: 'Let him enter and come to me; I've been waiting for him for several days.'

The old man was called; he entered the place where Quetzalcoatl was, and said to him: 'How are you, my son? I have brought a medicine for you to drink.' Quetzalcoatl replied: 'Welcome, old man, I've been waiting for you for several days.' He asked Quetzalcoatl: 'How are you, how is your health?' Quetzalcoatl replied: 'I am very poorly; my whole body hurts; I can't move my feet or hands.'

A fanciful engraving depicting offerings to Quetzalcoatl (also opposite) of animal blood (piglet and fledglings) and human blood (by scarification of the ear and tongue).

So the old man said to the king: 'My lord, look at this; the medicine I've brought you is good and beneficial; whoever drinks it feels drunk; if you want to drink of it, it will intoxicate you while healing you, softening your heart and turning your thoughts to the distressing fatigues of death, or of your departure.'

Quetzalcoatl replied: 'Oh old man, where must I go?' The old man answered: 'You absolutely must go to Tullan-Tlapallan, where another old man awaits you; you will talk together, and, on your return, you will be changed into a youth; you will even return to a second childhood.'

On hearing these words, Quetzalcoatl's heart was filled with great emotion. The old man added: 'Lord, drink this medicine.' 'I don't want to drink it,' said Quetzalcoatl. But the old man insisted: 'Drink, lord,' he said,

'because, if you don't, you'll want to do so later; raise it, at least, to your forehead and drink a drop of it.'

Quetzalcoatl tasted it, and then drank it, crying: 'What is it? It seems to be very good and tasty stuff; it's cured me; I'm not ill any more; my health has returned.' 'Another sip,' said the old man, 'Drink again, for it is good and you'll be better afterwards.'

So Quetzalcoatl drank again and got drunk. He began to cry sadly, and his softened heart abandoned itself to the idea of departing, and the old sorcerer's trickery, which had duped him, never let him shake off this thought.

The medicine that Quetzalcoatl drank was none other than the local white wine, made with magueys, called *teometl.*

Bernardino de Sahagún
Florentine Codex: General History of the Things of New Spain, c. 1580

Indigenous society

Aztec civilization had a rigorous social organization. At the top there reigned the tlatoani, *'he who speaks'; he was elected by his peers, the* tecutli, *the 'princes'. At the bottom were the* macehualli, *the 'common men', those who obeyed. In the middle, or on one side, quite separate – the* pochteca *traded and spied on the emperor's behalf; the artisans bore the name of the glorious ancestors:* tolteca.

The Toltec model

In the 16th century, after the Spanish conquest, Sahagún's informants gathered from the old Aztecs embellished accounts about prosperous and mythical Tula.

Truly they were all there together,
lived there together.
The remains of what they made and
  left behind
are still there and can be seen, among
  them
the works not finished, among them
the serpent columns, the round columns
  of serpents
with their heads resting on the ground,
their tails and rattles in the air.
The mountain of the Toltecs can be
  seen there
and the Toltec pyramids, the structures
of stone and earth, with stucco walls.

Temple of Tlahuizcalpantecuhtli, temple of the morning star, at Tula.

Two-headed serpent in jade and mosaic.

The remains of Toltec pottery also are
  there;
cups and pots of the Toltecs can be dug
  from the ruins;
Toltec necklaces are often dug from the
  earth,
and marvellous bracelets, precious green
  stones,
emeralds, turquoise....

The Toltecs were a skilful people;
all of their works were good, all were
  exact,
all well made and admirable.

Their houses were beautiful, with
  turquoise mosaics,
the walls finished with plaster,
clean and marvellous houses, which is
  to say,
Toltec houses, beautifully made,
beautiful in everything....

Painters, sculptors, carvers of precious
  stones,
feather artists, potters, spinners, weavers,
skilful in all they made, they discovered
the precious green stones, the turquoise;
they knew the turquoise and its mines,
  they found
its mines and they found the mountains
  hiding
silver and gold, copper and tin,
and the metal of the moon.

The Toltecs were truly wise;
they conversed with their own hearts....
They played their drums and rattles;
they were singers, they composed songs
and sang them among the people;
they guarded the songs in their
  memories,
they deified them in their hearts.

Quoted in Miguel León-Portilla
Aztec Thought and Culture
Translated by Jack Emory Davis, 1963

Warfare

*Tlacaélel, the brother of Moctezuma I,
sings the glory of Huitzilopochtli, the
divinity who gained ascendancy over
Quetzalcoatl and now encourages
the Aztecs in their warlike pursuits,
demanding from them in return a tribute
in blood, the 'War of the Flowers'.*

Huitzilopochtli, the young warrior,
who acts above! He follows his path!
'Not in vain did I dress myself in yellow
  plumes,
for I am he who has caused the sun to
  rise.'

You, ominous lord of the clouds,
one is your foot!
The inhabitants of the cold region of
  wings,
Your hand opens.

Near the wall of the region of heat,
feathers were given, they are scattering.
The war cry was heard ... Ea, ea!
My god is called the Defender of men.

Oh, now he moves on, he who is
  dressed in paper,
he who inhabits the region of heat;
  in the region of dust,

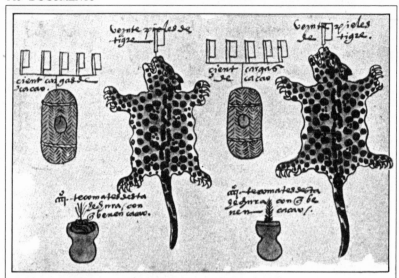

Items of tribute (above and opposite): jaguar skins, silos of maize.

---

he whirls about in the dust.
Those of Amantla are our enemies;
come and join me!
With struggle is war made;
come and join me!

Those of Pipiltlan are our enemies;
come and join me!
With struggle is war made;
come and join me!

Tlacáelel, speaking to Moctezuma I about the dedication of the Great Temple, remarked:

There shall be no lack of men to inaugurate the temple when it is finished. I have considered what later is to be done. And what is to be done later, it is best to do now. Our god need not depend on the occasion of an affront to go to war. Rather, let a convenient market be sought where our god may go with his army to buy victims and people to eat as if he were to go to a nearby place to buy tortillas ... whenever he wishes or feels like it. And may our people go to this place with their armies to buy with their blood, their heads, and with their hearts and lives, those precious stones, jade, and brilliant and wide plumes ... for the service of the admirable Huitzilopochtli.

This market, say I, Tlacaélel, let it be situated in Tlaxcala, Huexotzinco, Cholula, Atlixco, Tliluhquitépec and Tecóac. For if we situate it farther away, in such places as Yopitzinco or Michoacán or in the region of the Huaxtecs, all of which are already under our domination, their remoteness would be more than our armies could endure. They are too far, and, besides, the flesh of those barbaric people is not to the liking of our god. They are like old and stale tortillas, because, as I say, they speak strange languages and they are barbarians. For this reason it is more convenient that our fair and markets be in the six cities that I have mentioned.... Our god will feed himself with them as though he were eating warm tortillas, soft and tasty, straight out of the oven.... And this war should be of such a nature that we do not endeavour to destroy the others totally. War must always continue, so that each time and whenever we wish and our god wishes to eat and feast, we may go there as one who goes to market to buy something to eat ... organized to obtain victims to offer our god Huitzilopochtli.

Quoted in Miguel León-Portilla
Aztec Thought and Culture
Translated by Jack Emory Davis, 1963

Tribute

The subjects of the lords of Tenochtitlán paid all kinds of tribute – food, clothing, weapons.... The poorest among them, lacking what was necessary, offered their sons and daughters.

And as tribute they paid a great quantity of these feathers, feathers of all types and colours: green, blue, red, yellow, violet, white and mixed colours. Innumerable quantities of cacao; enormous quantities of cotton bales, both white and yellow.

As for blankets, there were an amazing number. There were some of twenty armspans, some of ten, five, four and two, according to what each province could manage. Lords' blankets, very rich, made in different methods and styles, so rich and so magnificent that some had great edgings worked with colour and feathers; others had great emblems; some had snake-heads,

Butterfly from the *Codex Sahagún*.

others lion-heads, and others depictions of the sun. On others were skulls, blowpipes, idols; all were worked with threads of various colours and mingled with duck and goose feathers, those tiny velvety feathers, superb and strange.

Although they had no silk in this country, there were clothes made of worked and painted cotton, of great curiosity and beauty, made with great care and elegance. There were also blankets of agave thread, with which the Chichimecs paid tribute, worked and painted in colours with immense delicacy, decorated with emblems of golden eagles and a thousand other weapons and insignia; of these there were huge quantities.

These nations paid tribute to the Mexicans with live birds, the most precious kinds with rich plumage; some green, others red or blue; parrots, big and small, and all kinds of elegant coloured birds, eagles, eagle-owls, sparrow-hawks, kestrels, crows, herons, geese, big goslings.

There were wild animals of all kinds: tribute was paid with live lions and tigers, and wild cats; all kinds of wild animals; they were brought in cages. Then snakes, big and small, poisonous and non-venomous, wild and tame.... It was really something to see, in cooking pots, all the kinds of serpents and creatures they paid tribute with! Even centipedes, scorpions, spiders, they asked for them in tribute, thus making themselves lords of every creature; everything was theirs, and belonged to them!

And what about the people on the coast? Every type of shell produced by the sea was brought in tribute: pectines, snails, big and little; curious fish-bones, carapaces of freshwater and marine turtles, big and small; stones from the sea, pearls, amber and granite; red and yellow, green, blue, violet and pale green; all kinds of colours, scarlet, alum, some *nacazcolotl*, and some *zacatlaxcalli*, which are plants with which they make colours, vitriol, dye-wood.

Other provinces paid tribute with hollow cups, big and small, some plain, others worked and others gilded and painted in rich and curious designs that still survive: some are worked superbly. They also paid with big plain bowls which they have like we have silver plates, or big plates for carrying food to the table and for offering water to rinse the hands. They also gave handled cups, very surprising, like little cauldrons. In any case, they paid tribute with these cups and bowls of all kinds, big and medium, small and even smaller, made in different ways and styles of workmanship, and different shapes and colours.

Others paid tribute with women's clothing, blouses and skirts, as superb

Estas Plumas ô las Vanderas eran señal de Tributo Real encima de los tercios ô petacas.

Adornos   Militares.

Centzontli Nacazminqui.   Centzontli Tenchapanqui.
400. Mantas redondas.   400. Mantas guarnecidas en la orla.

Centzontli Canauac.
400 Mantas finas.

Some of the riches paid in tribute: feather crowns, clothing, mats.

and elegant as they could make them, full of wide edgings, astonishingly worked with various colours and designs, and feathers on the chest, wide emblems drawn with coloured thread and, on the back, on others, they put worked roses; on yet others, imperial eagles; others were overlain with worked flowers so intermingled with feathers that they were a joy to see. Extremely rich skirts in price and value, superbly woven with excellent guile. Clothes that were worn by the wives and women of the lords and great men.

There was another type of women's clothing that was paid in tribute; all white, it was for the young and old women who served in the temples. Another type of garment for women, woven with agave thread, was distributed to servants. Mats of different kinds and designs were brought as tribute from other provinces; some of palms, others of furze; yet others made

of broad and very shiny straw; other mats were made of canes, others of marsh-rushes. Tribute was also paid with seats, in the same way as with mats, with backs that were chiselled and worked with great elegance.

From other provinces tribute was paid with maize and beans, with *chia* [a type of sage], with *huauhtli* [amaranth] and with pimentos of different species and kinds that exist and are cultivated in this land, and which are used for the different types and methods of stews they cook, by which they are differentiated and named. Great quantities of gourd-pips were paid in tribute.

From other places, tribute was paid in cut wood, and tree bark which was used as fuel by the lords because of the fine embers it makes, and tribute was also paid with a great amount of charcoal which came from all peoples who lived near mountains.

Other people paid tribute in stone, lime, wood, planks and beams for building their houses and temples. From other regions and provinces were brought deer, rabbits and quails, some fresh, others roasted. Tribute was paid with moles, weasels and big mice that we call rats, which are raised in the mountains.

Others paid tribute with grilled crayfish and ants, those big winged ants, and crickets, and all the tiny creatures that live on the earth. Thus, those living near lagoons paid tribute with all that grows in and around lagoons, even the silt and the flies that wander above, up to and including the water-mites and worms.

Then the peoples who had fruits, as was the case in the region of the Tierra Caliente, paid tribute with all the kinds of fruit there are in these provinces: pineapples, bananas, anonas, marmalade plums. In others, a thousand kinds of sapodillas, and goodies produced in these provinces from guavas, yellow, black and white plums, avocados and potatoes of two or three kinds.

These provinces paid tribute every day with great loads of roses, made and prepared with a thousand different kinds, because in Tierra Caliente there are very many types with a very strong perfume, some better than others, with a delicate perfume. They also brought the trees of these roses, with their roots, to plant them in the lords' houses, and all this was a tribute meant only to display the Mexicans' grandeur and authority, and show that the lords had power to name and keep all that is created in water as well as on land.

So much for clothing and food; but there were provinces that paid tribute in armour made of cotton, very well stuffed and padded so that neither arrows nor spears could pierce them; shields made of woven sticks, so solid and thick that a sword could not make a hole in them. The front of these shields was very elegantly decorated with feathers of all colours.... Very beautiful armour, and depictions of ancient feats by their ancient lords and idols, which they use and still keep today in memory of their antiques and past deeds and lords.

They paid tribute with big and thick bows; arrows of different kinds and types. They paid tribute with very well worked round-stones for slings, and with innumerable slings; white and black blades for swords; flints for arrowheads and darts.

Finally, imagine everything imaginable that there could be in this land from which tribute was paid to Mexico. Including honeycombs and the very bees in their hives; big jars of white honey and the other brown kind; tree resin, torches for illumination; soot, for smearing oneself, and roucou. And those provinces lacking in provisions, clothing and all the above, paid tribute with young women, girls and boys, which the lords shared among themselves. The males were called 'slaves', the females were almost all taken as concubines and gave birth to the sons of slaves, to which some people refer. In their quarrels over claims, when they are at the end of their tether, they leave and put a stop to it by saying, 'He's the son of a slave'. And this means those born of these concubines who, in ancient times, were the tribute of certain peoples.

Diego Durán
The History of the Indies of New Spain
1581

The market of Tlatelolco

In 1519 Cortés entered Great Mexico, which at the time included both Tenochtitlán and Tlatelolco, accompanied by his armed guards. He never wearied of admiring its wealth. Bernal Díaz del Castillo, Cortés' constant companion, gave the following report.

On reaching the market-place ... we were astounded at the great number of people and the quantities of merchandise, and at the orderliness and good arrangements that prevailed, for we had never seen such a thing before. The chieftains who accompanied us pointed everything out. Every kind of merchandise was kept separate and had its fixed place marked for it.

Let us begin with the dealers in gold, silver, and precious stones, feathers, cloaks, and embroidered goods, and male and female slaves who are also sold there. They bring as many slaves to be sold in that market as the Portuguese bring Negroes from Guinea. Some are brought there attached to long poles by means of collars round their necks to prevent them from escaping, but others are left loose. Next there were those who sold coarser cloth, and cotton goods and fabrics made of twisted thread, and there were chocolate merchants with their chocolate. In this way you could see every kind of merchandise to be found anywhere in New Spain, laid out in the same way as goods are laid out in my own district of Medina del Campo, a centre for fairs, where each line of stalls has its own particular sort. So it was in this great market. There were those who sold sisal cloth and ropes and the sandals they wear on their feet, which are made from the same plant. All these were kept in one part of the market, in the place

Aztec merchants: on the way to town (top); installed at Tlatelolco (above).

assigned to them, and in another part were skins of jaguars and lions, otters, jackals, and deer, badgers, mountain cats, and other wild animals, some tanned and some untanned, and other classes of merchandise.

There were sellers of kidney-beans and sage and other vegetables and herbs in another place, and in yet another they were selling fowls, and birds with great dewlaps (turkeys), also rabbits, hares, deer, young ducks, little dogs, and other such creatures. Then there were the fruiterers; and the women who sold cooked food, flour and honey cake, and tripe, had their part of the market. Then came pottery of all kinds, from big water-jars to little jugs, displayed in its

Customers and merchants under the arcades of the market at Tlatelolco in the pre-hispanic period.

own place, also honey, honey-paste, and other sweets like nougat. Elsewhere they sold timber too, boards, cradles, beams, blocks, and benches, all in a quarter of their own.

Then there were the sellers of pitch-pine for torches, and other things of that kind, and I must also mention, with all apologies, that they sold many canoe-loads of human excrement which they kept in the creeks near the market. This was for the manufacture of salt and the curing of skins, which they say cannot be done without it. I know that many gentlemen will laugh at this, but I assure them it is true. I may add that on all the roads they have shelters made of reeds or straw or grass so that they can retire when they wish to do so, and purge their bowels unseen by passers-by, and also in order that their excrement shall not be lost.

But why waste so many words on the goods in their great market? If I describe everything in detail I shall never be done. Paper, which in Mexico they call *amatl*, and some reeds that smell of liquidambar, and are full of tobacco, and yellow ointments and other such things, are sold in a separate part. Much cochineal is for sale too, under the arcades of that market, and there are many sellers of herbs and other such things. They have a building there also in which three judges sit, and there are officials like constables who examine the merchandise. I am forgetting the sellers of salt and the makers of flint knives, and how they split them off the stone itself, and the fisherwomen and the men who sell small cakes made from a sort of weed which they get out of the great lake, which curdles and forms a kind of bread which tastes rather like cheese. They sell axes too, made of bronze and copper and tin, and gourds and brightly painted wooden jars.

We went on to the great temple, and as we approached its wide courts, before leaving the market-place itself, we saw many more merchants who, so I was told, brought gold to sell in grains, just as they extract it from the mines. This gold is placed in the thin quills of the large geese of that country, which are so white as to be transparent. They used to reckon their accounts with one another by the length and thickness of these little quills, how much so many cloaks or so many gourds of chocolate or so many slaves were worth, or anything else they were bartering. Now let us leave the market, having given it a final glance....

Bernal Díaz del Castillo
The Conquest of New Spain
Translated by J. M. Cohen, 1963
Originally written c. 1568

The arts in Aztec society

Pre-hispanic Aztec society had a great number of categories of artist. Sahagún's informants collected songs of praise to their glory. Here are four of them....

The feather artist
Amantécatl: the feather artist.
He is whole; he has a face and a heart.

The good feather artist is skilful,
is master of himself; it is his duty
to humanize the desires of the people.
He works with feathers,
chooses them and arranges them,
paints them with different colours,
joins them together.

The bad feather artist is careless;
he ignores the look of things,
he is greedy, he scorns other people.
He is like a turkey with a shrouded heart,
sluggish, coarse, weak.
The things that he makes are not good.
He ruins everything that he touches.

The painter
The good painter is a Toltec, an artist;
he creates with red and black ink,
with black water....

Tarascan utensils.

Fresco by Diego Rivera from 1942 depicting the arts of Tarascan civilization: colouring fabrics, painting frescos, making a codex.

The good painter is wise,
God is in his heart.
He puts divinity into things;
he converses with his own heart.

He knows the colours, he applies
  them and shades them;
he draws feet and faces,
he puts in the shadows, he achieves
  perfection.
He paints the colours of all the flowers,
as if he were a Toltec.

The potter
He who gives life to clay:
his eye is keen, he moulds
and kneads the clay.

The good potter:
he takes great pains with his work;
he teaches the clay to lie;
he converses with his heart;
he makes things live, he creates them;
he knows all, as though he were a
  Toltec;

he trains his hands to be skilful.
The bad potter:
careless and weak,
crippled in his art.

The smith
Here it is told
how a work was cast
by the smiths of precious metals.
They designed, created, sketched it
with charcoal and wax, in order
to cast the precious metal,
the yellow or the white;
thus they began their works.

If they began the figure of a living thing,
if they began the figure of an animal,
they searched only for the similarity;
they imitated life
so that the image they sought
would appear in the metal.

Perhaps a Huaxtec,
perhaps a neighbour
with a pendant hanging from his nose,
his nostrils pierced, a dart in his cheek,
his body tattooed with little obsidian
   knives;
thus the charcoal was fashioned,
was carved and polished....

Whatever the artist makes
is an image of reality;
he seeks its true appearance.

If he makes a turtle,
the carbon is fashioned thus:
its shell as if it were moving,
its head thrust out, seeming to move,
its neck and feet
as if it were stretching them out.

If it is a bird
that is to be made of the precious metal,
then the charcoal is carved

Hammering a piece of metal.

to show the feathers and the wings,
the tail-feathers and the feet.

If it is a fish,
then the charcoal is carved
to show the scales and fins,
the double fin of the tail.
Perhaps it is a locust or a small lizard;
the artist's hands devise it,
thus the charcoal is carved.

Or whatever is to be made,
perhaps a small animal, or a golden
   neckpiece
with beads as small as seeds
around its border,
a marvellous work of art,
painted and adorned with flowers.

Quoted in Miguel León-Portilla
Aztec Thought and Culture
Translated by Jack Emory Davis, 1963

Human sacrifices

Aztec pictograms, Aztec oral tradition, the chronicles of the Spanish conquerors: they all agree that mass human sacrifice was an accepted and common practice among the Aztecs. How and why? Here are an account from the time of the conquest and two attempts at interpretation by modern authors.

On the horrible human sacrifices practised by the Aztecs

The people of Piru may well have had the edge over those of Mexico in killing children and sacrificing their sons – for I have neither read nor heard that the Mexicans had this custom – but in the number of men they sacrificed and in the horrible way they did it they surpassed the people of Piru and indeed all the nations of the world. And to show the state of blind misfortune in which the devil kept these people, I shall refer at length to the inhuman practice they had in these regions.

Firstly, the sacrificed men were obtained through war, and they did not perform these solemn sacrifices if there were no captives, and that is why, according to some authors, the sacrifices were called victims, because they were defeated; the sacrifice was also called *hostia, quasi ab hoste*, because it was an offering made by one's enemies, although the use of the two terms was extended to all manner of sacrifice. In fact, the Mexicans only sacrificed their captives to their idols; and their wars were usually waged to obtain captives for their sacrifices.

Hence, when they fought each other, they tried to keep their adversaries alive, to take them without killing them, in order to enjoy their sacrifice, and that was the reason given by Moctezuma to the Marquis del Valle when asked why, having such power and having conquered so many kingdoms, he had not subjugated the province of Tlaxcala, which was so close. Moctezuma replied to this that there were two reasons to explain why they had not pacified this province, which they could easily have done had they wished.

The first was to have something to

exercise Mexican youth, to prevent it being raised in idleness and pleasure; the second and main reason was that he had reserved this province as a source of captives to sacrifice to their gods.

The method adopted for these sacrifices was that on this palisade of skulls ... they grouped those who were to be sacrificed, and at the foot of this palisade they carried out a ceremony with them, which involved putting them all in single file at the foot of it, with many guards surrounding them.

Then a priest would come out, dressed in an alb with a fringed hem, and he came down from the temple summit with an idol made of white-beet and maize mixed with honey, its eyes made of green pearls, and its teeth of maize-seeds; he came down the temple steps as fast as he could, and climbed on to a great stone fixed on a very big cross in the middle of the court. This stone was called *quauhxicalli*, which means stone of the eagle.

The priest climbed up a little staircase in front of the cross and descended another on a different side, still with the idol in his arms; he then climbed up to where those to be sacrificed were located, and he went from one side to the other, showing this idol to each man, saying: 'This one is your god.' When he had finished showing it to them, he descended the steps at the other side, and all those who were to die departed in procession to the place where they were to be sacrificed. There they found ready the ministers who were to sacrifice them.

The usual method of sacrifice was to open the victim's chest, pull out his heart while he was still half-alive, and then knock down the man, rolling him down the temple steps which were awash with blood.

To understand this better, you must know that, at the place of sacrifice, six

The Great Temple of Tenochtitlán, at the top of which sacrificial rites (opposite) took place.

sacrificers came and were installed in this high rank; four to hold the victim's feet and hands, another for the throat, and one to cut the chest and extract the victim's heart. They were called *chachalmua*, which in our language is the same thing as minister of sacred things; this was a supreme rank, held in very high esteem among them, and inherited like a property.

The minister who had the function of killing, the sixth of the group, was considered and revered as a supreme priest or pontiff, whose name varied according to the period or the solemnities during which sacrifices were made; also, their vestments were different when they came out to exercise their office, varying with the moment. The man of this rank was *papa* and *topilzin*; the costume and vestments were a red tunic of dalmatic style, with a fringed hem; a crown of rich green and yellow feathers on the head, and, in the ears, a kind of gold ring set with green stones; and under the lips, towards the middle of the chin, a piece of blue stone....

These six sacrificers came out, their face and hands coated in a very dark black; five had a very crimped and tangled hairstyle with bands of leather attached around the head, and on their forehead they wore small discs of paper painted in several colours; they were clothed in white dalmatics worked in black. With this ornamentation they were dressed like the devil, and to see them come out with such an evil appearance frightened the people immensely.

The supreme priest carried in his hand a big flint knife, very pointed and wide; another priest carried a necklace of worked wood that looked like a snake. All six stood before the idol, prostrated themselves, and lined up near the pyramidal stone I described above as being just in front of the door of the idol's chamber. This stone was so pointed that when a sacrificial victim was thrown on his back against it, he was bent over in such a way that in dropping the knife to his chest it was very easy to open him up the middle.

Once these sacrificers were placed in order, they brought out all those who had been taken prisoner in the wars who were to be sacrificed at these festivals; accompanied closely by guards, they were made to climb those long staircases, all in rows, and totally naked, up to the place where one could see the ministers. As they arrived in order, they were each taken by the six sacrificers, one by the foot, another by the other foot, one by the hand and another by the other, and were thrown on their back against this pointed stone, where the fifth minister threw the necklace round their throat, and the sovereign priest opened their chest with this knife, with a strange quickness, pulling out their heart with his hands and showing it, still steaming, to the sun, and offering it this heat and steam. Then he turned to the idol, and threw it in its face; then they threw the victim's body down the temple steps; it rolled very easily because the stone was so close to the steps that there was not even two feet of space between the stone and the first step; hence, with a kick they threw the corpses down the steps.

In the same way they sacrificed all those available, one by one, and after they were dead and their corpses thrown down, they were picked up by their owners, the people who had actually captured them; they carried them off

Human sacrifice.

and shared them out and ate them, celebrating the ceremony with them; there were always more than forty or fifty of them, because they were men who were very skilled at taking prisoners. All the other neighbouring nations did the same thing, thus imitating the Mexicans in their rituals and their ceremonies in the service of their gods.

José de Acosta
Natural and Moral History of the Indies
1590

Two modern assessments of the Aztecs' ritual sacrifice

Soustelle's teleological viewpoint postulates the complete oneness of the sacrificial act with its ideological representation: human blood, food of the sun-god, is the driving force behind the universe of men.

One has to say that the extent of bloody rituals in Mexico, far from stemming from an innate and continually increasing cruelty, on the contrary coincides with a social and cultural evolution marked by a softening of manners. This is certainly a paradox, but one which has to be faced because it is based on facts which are certainly known. Yet one must try to understand. To do this means escaping as far as one can from the gravitational field of our own civilization, and placing ourselves in the minds of the ancient Mexicans.

What dominates this universe, what penetrates its whole conception, is the idea that the machinery of the world, the sun's movement, the succession of the seasons, cannot be maintained and cannot last unless they are nourished with the vital energy held in 'precious water', *chalchiuatl*, that is, human blood....

Four worlds, the four suns, have already perished before ours in cataclysms, and the one in which we live will also succumb. So men – more especially the people of the sun, the Aztec tribe – have to carry out a cosmic mission, to repulse day after day the assault of annihilation. And it is a miracle renewed at every dawn which makes the sun rise up once again – provided that the warriors and priests have offered its 'nourishment', *tlaxcaltiliztli*, the blood and hearts of the sacrificed.

The idea therefore – pushed rigorously to its most extreme and (for us) monstrous consequences, but with a perfectly coherent logic – that led to this bloody civilization was not based on a more inhuman or more cruel psychological foundation than other cosmological ideas. What our minds find difficult to grasp is the link – apparently obvious and indisputable for the peoples of late Mexico – between the continuity of natural phenomena and the offering of blood. But we have to accept this notion as 'given' in the same way as the shape of the house, ornament or garment that characterize one culture and not another, or the choice of the phonemes used by one language and not its neighbour. There is no necessity about it: it is only one of the very numerous ways in which man, faced with the mysteries of his own destiny, tries to comprehend them in order to extract from this vision a rule of action. All we can say is that, after a certain period, some peoples chose this *Weltanschauung* among all those that were possible, whereas the peoples of the preceding phase, those of Teotihuacán and Palenque, had chosen another....

It would clearly be ridiculous to try and explain such 'superstructures' (to use Marxist terminology), through economic and social 'infrastructures'.

Jacques Soustelle
The Four Suns, 1967

The metaphysical explanation of human sacrifice leaves many specialists perplexed. Couldn't there be other causes – material, economic, demographic – at the origin of this butchery?

Without seeking to find a single explanation of human sacrifice – an enterprise obviously doomed to failure – we can nevertheless place the emergence of systematic sacrificial practices in the central plateau in its wider context. As far as one can judge from historical and archaeological data, it seems to coincide with two contemporary events: on the one hand, the new arrivals reached the edges of Tula and found themselves in the presence of staked-out lands that had long been occupied by sedentary agriculturalists; deprived of pasture-lands, the former hunters were inescapably led to engage in a struggle against the indigenous owners. On the other hand, at the entrance of the immense northern plains, the outskirts of the Valley of Mexico represent a narrow bottleneck; the territory shrinks, and demographic concentration increases. The ancient rivalries between Chichimec tribes, which previously found their solution in dispersal and reciprocal distancing, could not fail to be exacerbated in a context that necessarily tended towards promiscuity. For all these populations of immigrants from the north, the struggle for living space had to be fought on two fronts: against the rival tribes, and against the original inhabitants. This continued until the *pax azteca* war was endemic throughout the *altiplano*. Human sacrifice, which is an appendage of war elevated into a system, quite naturally became its validation and ideological justification.

Christian Duverger
The Origin of the Aztecs, 1983

Temple of the sun (below) at the top of which was the stone of sacrifices (right).

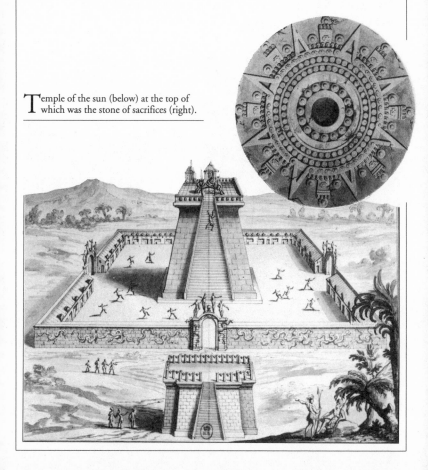

The rough and smooth of the conquest

March 1519: Cortés reaches the coast of Yucatán. 8 November 1519: the Spaniards make a triumphant entry into Tenochtitlán. Driven out again on 30 June 1520, they besiege it on 30 May 1521. On 13 August the Aztecs capitulate.

Death of Moctezuma II, killed by his own people, according to Spanish legend.

Visions, dreams and a meeting

Shortly before the Spaniards arrived, the whole Triple Alliance rumbles with stories announcing the imminent end of the reign of Moctezuma. Of all these bad forebodings, that of the stone of sacrifice of the flayed men is among the most famous.

He asked the king of Azcapotzalco for reinforcements and, when they arrived with their coils of rope and their tools, everyone began to pull, but the stone, without moving or giving the slightest sign of wanting to, again spoke: 'Poor wretches, why do you work in vain? Haven't I told you that I won't reach Mexico? Go and tell Moctezuma that there is no more time; he has delayed too long in making up his mind. Tell

The king of Texcoco, Nezahualpilli, announces the Spaniards' arrival to Moctezuma.

him that he should have set about it earlier if he wanted to carry me off; I no longer need to go, because something else has been determined by divine wish. He should not oppose his destiny. Why should I go over there? To be subject afterwards to ruin and contempt? Warn him that his power and his rule are ending, that he will soon see and experience for himself the end that awaits him for having wished to be greater than the god himself who determines things. So leave me because, if I start to move, it will be the worse for you.'

Moctezuma did not wish to give any credence to the tale which was related to him, although he was starting to feel some fear.

But soon there could no longer be any doubt. Everything, including the dreams of the old men themselves, agreed in predicting the arrival of the strangers and the end of Moctezuma. Could soothsayers and sorcerers confirm the disastrous omen?

The governors and village chiefs ... sent numerous soothsayers, sorcerers, magicians and enchanters who presented themselves to him and said, 'Lord, we came at your beckoning to learn your wishes and see what you want of us.' He replied, 'Be welcome. You must know the reason why I've called you, I want to know if you've seen or heard or dreamed something concerning my kingdom and my person, since you are skilled at probing nocturnal space, travelling over mountains, piercing the enigmas of the waters, and scrutinizing the movements of the heavens and the course of the stars. I beg you to hide nothing from me, and to speak to me openly.'

They answered: 'Lord, who would be so impudent as to lie in your presence? We have neither seen nor heard nor dreamed anything concerning what you ask.'

Moctezuma became angry, and said: 'So your profession is to be swindlers, liars, to pretend that you're men of science and that you know the future, to trick everyone by claiming that you know everything that happens in the universe, that you have access to what is locked in the heart of mountains and at the centre of the earth, that you see what is under the water, in caves and the fissures of the soil, in holes and in the gushing of fountains. You pretend to be children of the night, and all is lies and falsehood.' And, in a terrible rage, he called his men at arms, and ordered them to throw them into cages and have them watched by a strong guard so they could not escape.

In prison these soothsayers and sorcerers did not show any despair but were full of joy and happiness, and they continually laughed among themselves. Moctezuma was informed of this and sent his officers to beg them to confess what they knew, promising them their freedom. They replied that, since he was so insistent on knowing his misfortune, they would tell him what they had learned from the stars in heaven and all the sciences in their power; that he was to be the victim of so astonishing a wonder that no man had ever known a similar fate. And, venting his anger and his ire, one of the oldest prisoners cried to everyone: 'Let Moctezuma know that in a single sentence I want to tell him what will become of him. Those who are to avenge the affronts and sufferings he has inflicted and is inflicting on us are already on the march. And I will say nothing more, being content to await what must happen very soon.'

Hence, when his informers warn him of the landing of Cortés' small troop, Moctezuma, convinced that he is dealing with gods, hurries to go and meet them.

When it was announced to him that Cortés' arrival was imminent, he had

The meeting: Moctezuma, perched on a palanqui

himself raised again on to the shoulders of the princes, as he had come, and went to meet him. Then, seeing the marquis, he slid from his hammock and stepped to the ground. Seeing this, Hernán Cortés dismounted from the horse on which he had come, and went to embrace him with great reverence. King Moctezuma did the same and welcomed him with humility and deference. And taking from the hands of one of the

neath a canopy, receives Cortés and his men.

was beside the road, and where the powerful king and the marquis sat down on chairs prepared for them. Then the two other kings presented themselves, those of Texcoco and of Tacuba; one after the other they kissed the marquis' hands and offered him their necklaces and their roses, in accordance with their rank. And after them there came all the great men of the kingdom, making the same ceremonies and the same bows as to their god Huitzilopochtli.

Once this long and painstaking salutation was over, Moctezuma addressed the marquis, using Marina as interpreter, and bid him welcome in his city: he greatly rejoiced at his presence and at the sight of him, and recalled that he had replaced him on the throne and had governed the kingdom that his father, the god Quetzalcoatl, had left, holding – although unworthy to do so – the reins of power and receiving, in his name, the allegiance of his vassals; and if now the god was coming to reclaim his throne, he placed himself in his service and gladly abdicated, because the prophecies and tales of his ancestors had announced and promised this to him; let him recover his rights, if he so desired, Moctezuma would submit to his power; but if he had only come to visit him, he thanked him very sincerely and assured him that, to the bottom of his heart, he felt an intense pleasure and extreme joy because of this; he should rest and ask whatever he needed, his vassal would provide him with it in abundance.

Moctezuma affirmed his obedience, placing himself in his hands and in the service of His Majesty from that moment on, and he expressed his desire to be instructed in the holy Catholic faith. And hence, after this long halt in

kingdom's nobles a very rich golden necklace, made of numerous plaques of gold and set with precious stones, he placed it round his neck and put in his hand a strange and superb plume of feathers worked into the shape of a rose. He also placed a garland of roses round his neck, and put on his head a crown of roses; then, taking each other by the hand, they went together to the sanctuary of the goddess Toci, which

this sanctuary or little temple, they left for the city of Mexico, the marquis on horseback and the powerful angry king carried in his palanquin as he had come, on the shoulders of his nobles.

Diego Durán
The History of the Indies of New Spain
1581

The taking of Tenochtitlán, as told by Hernán Cortés

Welcomed as a god, Cortés throws down the idols in the great temple. Although he obtains Moctezuma's allegiance, there are rumblings of rebellion in the city. He undertakes the military conquest of Tenochtitlán, an adventure which he narrates, in detail, to his sovereign, Charles V.

This great city of Tenochtitlán is built on the salt lake, and no matter by what road you travel there are two leagues from the main body of the city to the mainland. There are four artificial causeways leading to it, and each is as wide as two cavalry lances. The city itself is as big as Seville or Córdoba. The main streets are very wide and very straight; some of these are on the land, but the rest and all the smaller ones are half on land, half canals where they paddle their canoes. All the streets have openings in places so that the water may pass from one canal to another. Over all these

openings, and some of them are very wide, there are bridges....

Seeing that if the inhabitants of this city wished to betray us they were very well equipped for it by the design of the city, for once the bridges had been removed they could starve us to death without our being able to reach the mainland, as soon as I entered the city I made great haste to build four brigantines, and completed them in a very short time. They were such as could carry three hundred men to the land and transport the horses whenever we might need them....

There are, in all districts of this great city, many temples or houses for their idols. They are all very beautiful buildings.... Amongst these temples there is one, the principal one, whose great size and magnificence no human tongue could describe, for it is so large that within the precincts, which are surrounded by a very high wall, a town of some five hundred inhabitants could easily be built. All round inside this wall there are very elegant quarters with very large rooms and corridors where their priests live. There are as many as forty towers, all of which are so high that in the case of the largest there are fifty steps leading up to the main part of it; and the most important of these towers is higher than that of the cathedral of Seville....

There are three rooms within this great temple for the principal idols,

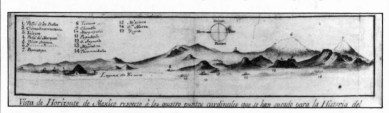

Vista de Horizonte de Mexico respecto á los quatro puntos cardinales que se han sacado para la Historia del

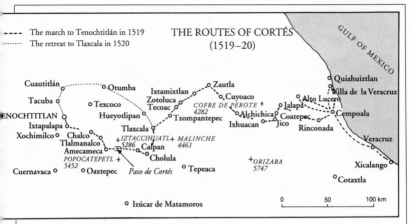

The Routes of Cortés (1519–20) map:

- - - - The march to Tenochtitlán in 1519
.... The retreat to Tlaxcala in 1520

THE ROUTES OF CORTÉS
(1519–20)

GULF OF MEXICO

Cuautitlán
Otumba
Ixtamixtlan
Zautla
Quiahuiztlan
Villa de la Veracruz
Tacuba
Texcoco
Zotoluca
Tecoac
Cuyoaco
COFRE DE PEROTE 4282
Alto Lucero
TENOCHTITLAN
Hueyotlipan
Tzompantepec
Jalapa
Cempoala
Ixtapalapa
Tlaxcala
Alchichica
Coatepec
Xochimilco   Chalco
Ixhuacan
Jico
Rinconada
Tlalmanalco
IZTACCIHUATL 5286
Calpan
MALINCHE 4461
Veracruz
Amecameca
Cholula
POPOCATEPETL 5452
Oaxtepec   Paso de Cortés
Tepeaca
ORIZABA 5747
Xicalango
Cuernavaca
Cotaxtla

Izúcar de Matamoros

0   50   100 km

which are of remarkable size and stature and decorated with many designs and sculptures, both in stone and in wood....

The most important of these idols, and the ones in whom they have most faith, I had taken from their places and thrown down the steps; and I had those chapels where they were cleaned, for they were full of the blood of sacrifices; and I had images of Our Lady and of other saints put there, which caused Moctezuma and the other natives some sorrow. First they asked me not to do it, for when the communities learnt of it they would rise against me, for they believed that those idols gave them all their worldly goods, and that if they were allowed to be ill treated, they would become angry and give them nothing and take the fruit from the earth, leaving the people to die of hunger. I made them understand through the interpreters how deceived they were in placing their trust in those idols which they had made with their hands from unclean things. They must know that there was only one God, Lord of all things, who had created heaven and earth and all else and who made all of us; and He was without beginning or end, and they must adore and worship only Him, not any other creature or thing ... and I urged them not to sacrifice living creatures to the idols, as they were accustomed, for, as well as being abhorrent to God, Your Sacred Majesty's laws forbade it and ordered that he who kills shall be killed. And from then on they ceased to do it, and in all the time I stayed in that city I did

The siege of Tenochtitlán. In this lakeshore city, built on a lagoon, whoever held the bridges would sooner or later be victorious.

not see a living creature killed or sacrificed.

Seventy-five days of siege and skirmishes....
Under the blows of Cortés, Aztec society
disintegrates; Moctezuma is killed. His
successor, Cuauhtémoc (Guatimozin),
soon has only a few faithful subjects
around him and eventually surrenders.

When it was light I had all the men made ready and the guns brought out. On the previous day I had ordered Pedro de Alvarado to wait for me in the market square and not to attack before I arrived. When all the men were mustered and all the brigantines were lying in wait behind those houses where the enemy was gathered, I gave orders that when a harquebus was fired they should enter the little of the city that was still left to win and drive the defenders into the water where the brigantines were waiting. I warned them, however, to look with care for Guatimozin, and to make every effort to take him alive, for once that had been

done the war would cease. I myself climbed onto a roof top, and before the fight began I spoke with certain chieftains of the city whom I knew, and asked them for what reason their lord would not appear before me; for, although they were in the direst straits, they need not all perish; I asked them to call him, for he had no cause to be afraid. Two of those chieftains then appeared to go to speak with him. After a while they returned, bringing with them one of the most important persons in the city, whose name was Ciguacoazin, and he was captain and governor of them all and directed all matters concerning the war. I welcomed him openly, so that he should not be afraid; but at last he told me that his sovereign would prefer to die where he was rather than on any account appear before me, and that he personally was much grieved by this, but now I might do as I pleased. I now saw by this how determined he was, and so I told him to return to his people and to prepare them, for I intended to attack and slay them all; and so he departed after having spent five hours in such discussions.

The people of the city had to walk upon their dead while others swam or drowned in the waters of that wide lake where they had their canoes; indeed, so

Outside the city, on open water, the Spanish brigantines, equipped with artillery, devastate the flotilla of Mexican canoes.

great was their suffering that it was beyond our understanding how they could endure it. Countless numbers of men, women and children came out towards us, and in their eagerness to escape many were pushed into the water where they drowned amid that multitude of corpses; and it seemed that more than fifty thousand had perished from the salt water they had drunk, their hunger and the vile stench. So that we should not discover the plight in which they were, they dared neither throw these bodies into the water where the brigantines might find them nor throw them beyond their boundaries where the soldiers might see them; and so in those streets where they were we came across such piles of the dead that we were forced to walk upon them. I had posted Spaniards in every street, so that when the people began to come out they might prevent our allies from killing those wretched people, whose number was uncountable. I also told the captains of our allies that on no account should any of those people be slain; but they were so many that we could not prevent more than fifteen thousand being killed and sacrificed that day.... When I saw that it was growing late and that they were not going to surrender or attack I ordered the two guns to be fired at them, for although these did some harm it was less than our allies would have done had I granted them licence to attack. But when I saw that this was of no avail I ordered the harquebus to be discharged, whereupon that corner which they still held was taken and its defenders driven into the water, those who remained surrendering without a fight.

Then the brigantines swept into that inner lake and broke through the fleet of canoes, but the warriors in them no longer dared fight. God willed that Garci Holguín, a captain of one of the brigantines, should pursue a canoe which appeared to be carrying persons of rank; and as there were two or three crossbowmen in the bows who were preparing to fire, the occupants of the canoe signalled to the brigantine not to shoot, because the lord of the city was with them. When they heard this our men leapt aboard and captured Guatimozin and the lord of Tacuba and the other chieftains with them. These they then brought to the roof close to the lake where I was standing, and as I had no desire to treat Guatimozin harshly, I asked him to be seated, whereupon he came up to me and, speaking in his language, said that he had done all he was bound to do to defend his own person and his people, so that now they were reduced to this sad state, and I might do with him as I pleased. Then he placed his hand upon a dagger of mine and asked me to kill him with it; but I reassured him saying that he need fear nothing. Thus, with this lord a prisoner, it pleased God that the war should cease, and the day it ended was Tuesday, the feast of Saint Hippolytus, the thirteenth of August, in the year 1521. Thus from the day we laid siege to the city, which was on the thirtieth of May of that same year, until it fell, there passed seventy-five days, during which time Your Majesty will have seen the dangers, hardships and misfortunes which these, Your vassals, endured, and in which they ventured their lives. To this, their achievements will bear testimony.

Hernán Cortés, *Letters from Mexico*
Translated and edited by Anthony R. Pagden, 1972

Cortés victorious at Tabasco, 18 March 1519.

The Aztecs, defeated but not enslaved

In June 1524, almost three years after the fall of Mexico, a meeting took place between the Aztec leaders and wise men and Cortés, who was surrounded by Franciscan missionaries. Although the vanquished made an act of allegiance, they nevertheless defended their spiritual values.

Our Lords, our very esteemed Lords:
great hardships have you endured to
  reach this land.
Here before you,
we ignorant people contemplate you....

Through an interpreter we reply,
we exhale the breath and the words
of the Lord of the Close Vicinity.
Because of Him we dare to do this.
For this reason we place ourselves in
  danger....

Perhaps we are to be taken to our ruin,
  to our destruction.
But where are we to go now?
We are ordinary people,
we are subject to death and destruction,
  we are mortals;
allow us then to die,

let us perish now,
since our gods are already dead....

You said
that we know not
the Lord of the Close Vicinity,
to Whom the heavens and the earth
    belong.
You said
that our gods are not true gods.
New words are these
that you speak;
because of them we are disturbed,
because of them we are troubled.
For our ancestors
before us, who lived upon the earth,
were unaccustomed to speak thus.
From them have we inherited
our pattern of life
which in truth did they hold;
in reverence they held,
they honoured, our gods.
They taught us
all their rules of worship,
all their ways of honouring the gods.
Thus before them, do we prostrate
    ourselves;
in their names we bleed ourselves;
our oaths we keep,
incense we burn,
and sacrifices we offer.

It was the doctrine of the elders
that there is life because of the gods;
with their sacrifice, they gave us life.
In what manner? When? Where?
When there was still darkness.

It was their doctrine
that they [the gods] provide our
    subsistence,
all that we eat and drink,
that which maintains life....

They themselves are rich,
happy are they,
things do they possess;

so forever and ever,
things sprout and grow green in their
    domain....
there 'where somehow there is life', in
    the place of Tlalocan.
There hunger is never known,
no sickness is there,
poverty there is not.
Courage and the ability to rule
they gave to the people....

And in what manner? When? Where
    were the gods invoked?
Were they appealed to; were they
    accepted as such;
were they held in reverence?

Above the world
they had founded
their kingdom.
They gave the order, the power,
glory, fame.

And now, are we
to destroy
the ancient order of life?
Of the Chichimecs,
of the Toltecs,
of the Acolhuas,
of the Tecpanecs?

We know
on Whom life is dependent;
on Whom the perpetuation of the race
    depends;
by Whom begetting is determined;
by Whom growth is made possible;
how it is that one must invoke,
how it is that one must pray.

Hear, oh Lords,
do nothing
to our people
that will bring misfortune upon them,
that will cause them to perish....

Calm and amiable,
consider, oh Lords,

whatever is best.
We cannot be tranquil,
and yet we certainly do not believe;
we do not accept your teachings as
    truth,
even though this may offend you.

Here are
the Lords, those who rule,
those who sustain, whose duty is to
the entire world.
Is it not enough that we have already
    lost,
that our way of life has been taken away,
has been annihilated.

Were we to remain in this place,
we could be made prisoners.
Do with us
as you please.

This is all that we answer,
that we reply,
to your breath,
to your words,
Oh, our Lords!

Quoted in Miguel León-Portilla
Aztec Thought and Culture
Translated by Jack Emory Davis, 1963

*Resistance to Christianity lasted for years,
as Andrés Mixcoatl's declaration before
the Tribunal of the Holy Office of the
Inquisition on 14 September 1537 reveals.*

My name is Andrés. I am a Christian.
A friar baptized me at Texcoco five
years ago. I don't know his name. I took
catechism every day at Texcoco with the
friars of St Francis and their disciples,
some young men in their charge. They
told us in their sermons to abandon our
idols, our idolatry, our rites; to believe
in God; and many other things. I
confess that, instead of practising what
they told me, for three years I have
preached and maintained that the

brothers' sermons were good for
nothing, that I was a god, that the
Indians should sacrifice to me and
return to the idols and sacrifices of the
past. During the rainy season, I made
it rain. That is why they presented me
with paper, copal, and many other
things, including property.

I often preached in plain daylight at
Tulancingo, Huayacocotla, Tututepec,
Apan, and many other places. It was at
Tepehualco, about four years ago, that
I became a god. Since there was no rain,
during the night I made magic
incantations with copal and other
things. The next day it rained a lot.
That is why they took me for a god.
The *chuchumecas* executed one of their
priests, claiming that he knew nothing
and couldn't make it rain, I declare that
when I engaged in these superstitions
and magic practices, the devil spoke to
me and said: 'Do this, do that'. At
Tepetlaoztoc I did the same thing....

Why do you abandon the things of
the past and forget them, if the gods that
you worshipped then looked after you
and gave you what you needed? You
must realize that everything the Brothers
say is mere lies and falsehoods. They
have brought nothing to look after you,
they don't know us, nor we them. Did
our fathers and grandfathers know these
monks? Did they see what they preach,
this god they talk of? Not at all! On the
contrary, they are tricking us. We eat
what the gods give us, it is they who
feed us, shape us and give us strength.
Do we know these Brothers? I intend
to perform these sacrifices, and I'm not
going to abandon the habit because of
these people!

Quoted in Serge Gruzinski
Man-Gods in the Mexican Highlands
Translated by Eileen Corrigan, 1989

Sorcery and syncretism under Spanish domination

Victory by force of arms never ensures the domination of souls. In the 16th and 17th centuries, offerings and devotion to the old tutelary divinities coexist strangely with worship of the Christians' one God....

Healers and sorcerers

Domingo Hernández was originally from Tlaltizapan, a village on the right bank of the Rio Yautepec. There he built up a reputation for holiness after he received from heaven the 'virtue of healing illnesses'. This was in the first years of the 17th century.

When he was at death's door, two people dressed in white tunics appeared to him and took him very far from there to another place where there was a sick man, and there they blew on him. Then they led him to another place where they found another sick man, and again they blew on him. They then told him:

'Let us return to your house for they already weep for you; rest now, for after tomorrow we will return for you.'

At that moment, as he came to, he noticed that his friends were weeping for him as if he were already dead.

The two people dressed in white returned three days later. Like the first time, they took him to see the two sick men, and they blew on him just like before. Meanwhile, they told him:

'Hurry if you want to see your parents, your grandparents and the rest of your family, but if they find you, you must absolutely not answer them; otherwise you will stay with them and you will not reach the world again.'

Then he saw two roads, one very wide which many people took – that of the damned – the other narrow and steep, full of brush, rushes and thorns. It was, they told him, the path of our Redeemer. He saw that few followed it, and again that many people took the broad path. The people in white tunics

ordered him to follow them, and they arrived at the houses of the prodigies, where they told him:

'*Xitlamahuico*, look, and pay attention to what you see. Observe what happens to those who get drunk; beware, don't start your drinking again ... (and many other things of that sort), otherwise you'll endure the same tortures. Give up pulque immediately (or) in three days you'll come back here. Now let's go to your house, for they are already weeping for you, and they should not be allowed to bury you.'

They then told him:

'Listen, you who are poor and miserable, here is what will give you food and drink in the world.'

They taught him the words ... which he has used ever since to care for people, and which brought him success in his treatments, even the most hazardous

Festival of pulque (agave beer), which the Mexicans have always used to get drunk.

ones. Whereupon they took him back to his house. There he came to, and noticed people weeping for him as if he were dead.

He then said that, this same night, three ladies magnificently dressed in white, and only in that colour, came to visit him, and he reported some of the words they had exchanged. According to him, it was the Virgin (Our Lady), Veronica and another lady whom he did not identify. Our Lady said that Christ Our Lord had captured this sick man, and she wanted to help him. Veronica obeyed her, and wafted some air to him with a piece of fabric. With that action he came to, and from that morning on he felt fine.

Hernando Ruiz de Alarcón
Treatise on Superstitions, 1629

The Spaniard and the sorcerer

Puebla, 1665. Testimony of a Spaniard from Huamantla in the trial of the 'idolatrous' Indians.

Six years ago, an Indian named Juan Coatl ('Cloud Serpent'), of the village of San Juan Ixtenco ... told me he wanted to make me rich, as he had done for others. To that end I was supposed to go with him to the Sierra of Tlaxcala, where he would give me a good deal of gold and silver – provided I kept a 'fast' consisting of staying away from women for two days before the Ascension. And in the event, driven by greed and curiosity to see whether the Indian would perform bad or superstitious acts, in the company of another Spaniard I climbed that mountain with Juan Coatl. When we got to a cabin that looked like a hermitage, the Indian lit candles and burned copal and incense in the hut.

Then, leaving me there, he told me to wait and disappeared into the mountain reaches. He returned after some time and reproached me for not having come in good faith, because I had broken the promised fast and because I had a brother in the Church. That is why he would not give me the money I had sent him to find; that is why the master of those parts (a divine being of some kind) was incensed. In spite of that, he would still get me quantities of things.

Seeing that the whole thing was a confidence game, I left the Indian. Four months later, I met him and asked why he had not kept his promise to make me rich, as he'd said he had done for others.

B aptisms, funerals and religious rites were all Christian ceremonies that still integrated traditional Indian practices after the Spanish conquest.

He answered that the mountain was very angry because one of my brothers was a priest, and to calm its wrath he had gone up another mountain called the Caldera. There his protector had appeared to him as he slept, telling him to get up and go tell the people of Huamantla and San Juan (Ixtenco) that he had calmed down and was no longer angry with them for having revealed his story: a heavy downpour that same day would be a sign. And if the Indian is to be believed, there really was a downpour.... I have heard the Indians say he is believed to be a high priest, that he marries and baptizes, choosing the name according to the day of birth on a calendar he has. He climbs to the Sierra of Tlaxcala with Indian men and women.

The truth according to the inquiry held by the ecclesiastical tribunal of the bishopric of Puebla.

Either by himself or with the intervention of some of the old fiscales of San Juan (Ixtenco), he gathers candles, copal, incense, and hens ... and he goes up to the Sierra, or mountain of Tlaxcala, where they say he has a cave beside the spring that flows to San Juan Ixtenco, by way of Canoas: two crosses mark the spot. At the entrance of the cave he lights candles, and inside he keeps idols, including a painted canvas representing an Indian woman with Indian youths at her feet, adoring her; another canvas delineating a figure with indigenous features, wearing a *tilma* (cape), with a stick in his hand; and two other paintings, one representing four snakes, and the other a large coiled serpent.... These are to be seen, along with other idols and a pile of garments offered in Juan Coatl's sanctuary....

Then he enters the cave with two other people, with lit candles and a great deal of copal. There they spend a day and a night in adoration of the idols ... for Juan Coatl tells them these are their real gods, who give them water and good crops and all the other goods they possess, that they should believe in them and in an idol that he shows them, saying that she is their Virgin. They must not believe in the God of the Spaniards or in the Blessed Virgin. The times they must go 'to the cave' he commands them to fast, which means abstaining from sleeping with their wives; and if by chance one of them disobeys, he treats them like 'dogs who do not fast'. One of them, among others, relates what happened to him for not having abstained on that occasion: when he returned to the village with him, Juan told him that he was nothing but a 'dirty dog of a drunkard' who did not come fasting. The others were amazed at what he knew about what everyone was doing. According to Coatl's wife, when he was about to go up the mountain he abstained the night before.

The Indians confessed, too, that when the parish priest came to the village, Juan reprimanded the children and adults who went to see him: why go to the priest, since he was more than the priest, he spoke with the gods and provided for them what they needed? And he repeated that they should not believe in God but in their idols.

Quoted in Serge Gruzinski
Man-Gods in the Mexican Highlands
Translated by Eileen Corrigan, 1989

Doctor and patient (above). Opposite: one of the many representations of the Virgin of Guadalupe (see also overleaf).

The healer and the Virgin

Yautepec, 11 September 1761: interrogation of Antonio Pérez, the 'shepherd' of the hamlet of Tlacoxcalco in the pueblo of Ecatzingo, aged forty, who was called shepherd 'because he once kept sheep'.

Four years ago, when I was living on the Gomez rancho at Tetizicayac in the jurisdiction of Atlatlahucan, I accompanied a Dominican father from there to the village of Yecapixtla. I do not know the name of the Dominican, where he comes from, or where he is. It could well be that he was the devil. I just remember that on the road the Dominican told me I was already

damned because I drank far too much.
Then he instructed me in caring for the
sick, advising me to use ... eggs, soap,
milk, cooking oil, mint, or tomato skins,
depending on the nature of the illness.
He taught me cures for everything,
including terrible toothaches, one of
which consisted of making vapours by
selecting six *tesontles* (volcanic rocks)
of the same size and sprinkling them
with water in which rue and artemisia
had been cooked. Then they had to be
taken and placed separately between
the patient's legs.

For all my treatments I recite the
Credo as the holy church teaches it
– in fact he was asked and was able to
say the prayer – and I add these words:
'In the name of the most holy Trinity,
of the Father, the Son and the Holy
Ghost. Amen.' I put my trust first in
God and only then in the herbs. When
he is on his way to recovery, the sick
man recites the act of contrition. I do
all that because the Dominican friar told
me to. That is how I cured Magdalena
from Tetelcingo of typhoid fever, my
wife Ana María of stomach pain, a
certain Domingo, whose name and
pueblo I do not know, of a leg wound....

For six *reales* I bought from a painter
named Bentura a very old painting, half
an ell in size, which represented Christ.
I kept it at my house and had it carefully
cleaned. Many people came to offer him
flowers and tapers. That is why Don
Jacinto Varela, the priest of
Atlatlahucan, had me arrested.
Afterwards he freed me so that I would
take him to my place and give him the
holy Christ. As I was getting ready to
do so, all of a sudden I found myself
with my painting in a cave at the
bottom of a ravine that runs along one
side of Atlatlahucan. I had been carried

there through the air, without knowing by whom, and I stayed in the cave for a moment before going to Chimalhuacan, where I gave the painting in question to the priest, who had it put under glass in his church. But since I accepted offerings of candles and money, the priest reprimanded me and put me out of the church.

Eight days later, in a place named Zabaleta, I met a *dieguino* [a barefoot Franciscan], who asked me to go with him to Puebla. I agreed, and all of a sudden found myself in the middle of the volcano, at the friar's side. The *dieguino* told me not to be sad about the holy Christ they had taken from me, because he would give me another, and in fact he gave me a head which seemed to be of glass, ordering me to make a body of cypress for it. I succeeded, with the help of a painter whose name I do not know, and I gave it the name of Santo Entierro [Christ of the Entombment]. I lit tapers before that Christ, recited some Credos and 'Glory be'. At the time of my arrest, I had that image at my house, and I do not know where it is now.

The same friar told me that in the volcano I would find a rainbow, and under the rainbow the Virgin; and that thereafter two new sources of water would appear at Chimalhuacan.

At the time, I disregarded his prediction and remained silent for a year and a half.

That time had passed when, sensing that I was giving up the ghost, I went to find Miguel Apparicio, Faustino, Antonio de la Cruz, and Pasqual de Santa María, to take them as witnesses to the cave. Once we got there, we saw a woman clad in a shining mantle and a body wrapped like a corpse. We did not

touch it, and it is still in that condition. We knelt and recited ten Credos before making an image of *ayacahuite*, to which we gave the epithets of the Light, of the Palm, of the Olive, and of the Lily. That is what the *dieguino* friar had specified when I had spoken with him. He had also ordered that we make the image along the lines of the one in the cave – that is, the body that appeared to be dead. We were supposed to take it to the church of Yautepec and then to the cave, where we would find all the instruments of the Passion. Thirty-seven men were to accompany me in the undertaking.

Although the image was not brought to the church, I did take it to the cave in the company of five people from Ecatzingo: my son Matheo, his brother Felipe, María, Theresa, Diego, and twenty-five others from Izamatitlan, among whom were the *fiscal* Pedro, Pasqual de Santa María, and others

whose names escape me. When we got there, I discovered all the instruments of the Passion in a hole; they were made of terracotta, and I took them home. Pasqual de Santa María took the Virgin to his place, and we recited the rosary before her, and the 'Glory be'; we danced and played music. That is what we were doing when the priest came in to arrest us.

Quoted in Serge Gruzinski
Man-Gods in the Mexican Highlands
Translated by Eileen Corrigan, 1989

Mexican 16th-century church in typical baroque style.

Greatness and misery of the descendants of the men-gods

Scattered and despoiled by four centuries of colonialism, the Indian and half-breed populations of the 20th century are squatters on the ever-expanding fringes of Mexico City. Today their future oscillates between extinction in the barren wilderness and emigration to the hostile megalopolis. As testimony to this, here are some statements by Indians collected by a Mexican ethnologist.

'Before, few people went to Mexico City because they didn't know it,' says Justino Esquivel. 'Now the people from Mexico City think we go to sell things there because we don't want to work; and they even throw petrol on our fruits; but we go out of necessity. As long as the government gives us no work, we'll be forced to go there....

'In the city they move us on, they punish us, and then they throw us in prison; but tough, if we're doing it out of necessity, we're going to carry on doing it. Under Uruchurtu [a mayor of the city known for his strict measures], as soon as they saw you in the street or sitting in a square, they took you: "Come on, to the clink with you! What are you doing there?" We have no papers. But when are they going to give us papers? They just have to see us (showing his old, worn-out clothes). Yes, we're not going to lie, look at us. Are you going to say we're rich? It's just that, here, there's no way out, that's why we go to Mexico City.'

Poor district of Mexico at the turn of the century.

On top of the difficulty of economic survival in the village, people stress the arduous nature of work in the fields, and the insecurity attached to it. One young man sums it up as follows:

'Here, there's no work, we earn nothing. We work with the boss from nine to nine, we sweat a lot to earn ten pesos. And the *zacatón* root [a type of Mexican fodder crop] is incredibly hard work. We start at six in the morning and get home at six in the evening, sometimes even at eight, completely covered in dust. It's a really filthy job....That's why we go to Mexico City and, God willing, we'll continue to go there, because here we earn nothing.'

The peasants of mixed origin, on the other hand, express other concerns.

'In twenty years time, nobody will be working the fields. I want a bit more for my children. They don't want to farm the land anymore, that's why we're leaving (for Mexico City). They need to study because employers now ask for the certificate of secondary studies for a regular job .... and here I can't give them all schooling (he has nine children), that's why I think I'm going to go to Mexico City.'

In general, the Mazahua peasants, especially those who haven't lived there, have a very favourable opinion of the city, the notorious myth that attracts migrants to urban centres.

'I would be happy to leave for Mexico City or somewhere else, because you can earn good money there....'

But success in the city remains something mysterious, something that cannot be understood.

'I don't know if it's luck, I don't know why, but there are people who go to Mexico City, and immediately they go up in the world. And things go well

for them. And there are others who stay a while and have to come back, they get nothing. Like me. I don't know if it's luck....' muttered one Indian.

Among migrants to the city, those who have succeeded in getting a decent income, and who have settled there, are happy they emigrated. In contrast, those who haven't found a permanent job and who live in great poverty in the seedy parts of town or the shanty towns complain bitterly about their situation.

Others, for their mental salvation, like those villagers who in their dreams make the city more beautiful, begin to imagine that village life is 'more beautiful'.

'If there was work at Dotejiare, I'd go back there. For most of the people there, things are all right, because they know how to run their affairs, they have good harvests.... The room where I live is lousy, it's better in Dotejiare. You're untroubled there, you have your house, even if it's small, you still have it....'

What emerges from this survey of different viewpoints is that the general tendency is not very subjective, except for the collection of myths exalting life in the city and in the countryside. For the most part they constitute fairly objective appreciations of the very concrete conditions that surround individuals. Hence, for example, the poorest Mazahua peasants do not even formulate a value judgment of migration; they limit themselves to putting it into practice.

Lourdes Arizpe
Migration, Ethnography and Economic Change, 1978

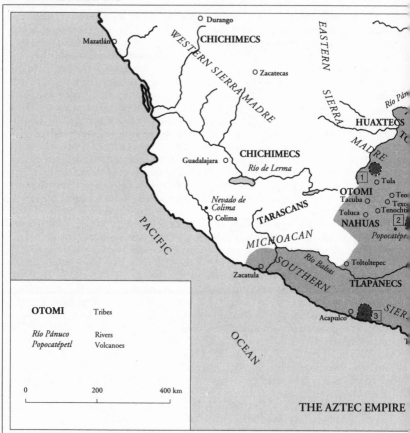

THE AZTEC EMPIRE

Map labels: Durango, Mazatlán, CHICHIMECS, WESTERN SIERRA MADRE, EASTERN, Zacatecas, SIERRA, Río Pán…, HUAXTECS, MADRE, CHICHIMECS, Guadalajara, Río de Lerma, Tula, OTOMI, Teo…, Tacuba, Texco…, Nevado de Colima, Colima, TARASCANS, Toluca, Tenochti…, NAHUAS, PACIFIC, MICHOACAN, Popocatépe…, Río Balsas, Toltoltepec, SOUTHERN, Zacatula, TLAPANECS, Acapulco, OCEAN, SIER…

Legend:
OTOMI — Tribes
Río Pánuco — Rivers
Popocatépetl — Volcanoes
0   200   400 km

FURTHER READING

Aveni, Anthony, *Empires of Time*, 1990
Berdan, Frances F., *The Aztecs of Central Mexico:
    An Imperial Society*, 1982
Bray, Warwick, *Everyday Life of the Aztecs*, 1968
Clendinnen, Inga, *Aztecs: An Interpretation*, 1991
Coe, Michael D., *Mexico*, 1984
Conrad, Geoffrey W., and Arthur A. Demarest,
    *Religion and Empire: The Dynamics of Aztec and
    Inca Expansionism*, 1984
Davies, Nigel, *The Aztecs: A History*, 1973
Diehl, Richard A., *Tula: The Toltec Capital of
    Ancient Mexico*, 1983
Durán, Diego, *The Aztecs: The History of the Indies
of New Spain* (original 1581), trans. Doris Heyden
    and Fernando Horcasitas, 1964
Fagan, Brian M., *Kingdoms of Gold, Kingdoms of Jade:
    The Americas before Columbus*, 1991
Farriss, Nancy M., *Maya Society under Colonial Rule:
    The Collective Enterprise of Survival*, 1984
Gibson, Charles, *The Aztecs under Spanish Rule:
    A History of the Indians of the Valley of Mexico,
    1519–1810*, 1964
Gillespie, Susan D., *The Aztec Kings: The Construction
    of Rulership in Mexica History*, 1989
Gruzinski, Serge, *Conquering the Indian Mind:
    The Making of Colonial Indian Cultures in Spanish
    Mexico, 16th-18th Centuries*, 1992
—, *Painting the Conquest: The Mexican Indians and the
    European Renaissance*, 1992

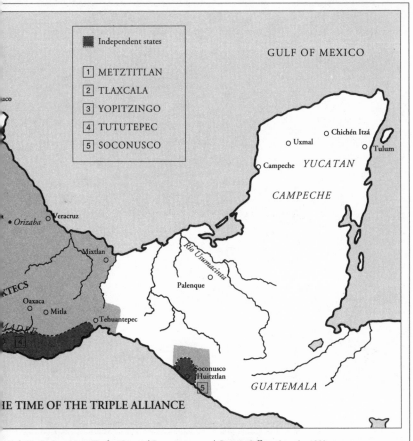

Independent states

1 METZTITLAN
2 TLAXCALA
3 YOPITZINGO
4 TUTUTEPEC
5 SOCONUSCO

GULF OF MEXICO

YUCATAN

o Chichén Itzá
o Uxmal
o Tulum
o Campeche
CAMPECHE

o Orizaba   o Veracruz
Mixtlan
Río Usumacinta

AZTECS
Oaxaca
o   o Mitla
o Tehuantepec
Palenque o

Soconusco
Huitztlan
5
GUATEMALA

THE TIME OF THE TRIPLE ALLIANCE

Hassig, Ross, *Aztec Warfare: Imperial Expansion and Political Control*, 1988
—, *Trade, Tribute and Transportation: The Sixteenth-Century Political Economy of the Valley of Mexico*, 1985
Lewis, Oscar, *The Children of Sánchez: Autobiography of a Mexican Family*, 1962
—, *Tepoztlán, Village in Mexico*, 1961
Lockhart, James, *Nahuas and Spaniards: Postconquest Central Mexican History and Philology*, 1991
Miller, Mary Ellen, *The Art of Mesoamerica: From Olmec to Aztec*, 1986
Moctezuma, Eduardo Matos, *The Great Temple of the Aztecs: Treasures of Tenochtitlán*, 1988
Ouwenweel, Arij, and Simon Miller (eds.), *The Indian Community of Colonial Mexico*, 1990

Parsons, Jeffrey, *Aztec Art*, 1983
Pasztory, Esther, *Aztec Art*, 1983
Paz, Octavio, *The Labyrinth of Solitude: Life and Thought in Mexico*, trans. Lysander Kemp, 1967
Ricard, Robert, *The Spiritual Conquest of Mexico*, trans. Lesley Byrd Simpson, 1966
Sabloff, Jeremy A., *The Cities of Ancient Mexico: Reconstructing a Lost World*, 1990
Soustelle, Jacques, *The Daily Life of the Aztecs*, 1961
Townsend, Richard F., *The Aztecs*, 1992
Weaver, Muriel Porter, *The Aztecs, Maya and their Predecessors*, 1981
White, Jon Manchip, *Cortés and the Downfall of the Aztec Empire*, 1971

Dates	Periods	Maya-Toltecs/Spaniards
650–950	Late Classic	**879** Date on a Maya lintel at Chichén Itzá
950–1200	Early Postclassic	**967** Quetzalcoatl leaves Tula for Chichén Itzá **End of the 10th or early 11th century** First 'Castillo' or temple-pyramid of Chichén Itzá **End of the 11th or early 12th century** Second Castillo **12th century** Ball game of Chichén Itzá **11th to the 13th centuries** Tikal is reoccupied **1194** Start of the league of Mayapán **12th century** End of Toltec domination in Yucatán
1200–1520	Late Postclassic	**13th century** Principal buildings at Tulum **1263** The Itzá found Mayapán **1283** Civil war with an Itzá lineage called Cocom **13th century** Construction of Mixco Viejo (Guatemala) **1441** End of the league of Mayapán **1470** Foundation of Iximché (Guatemala)
1520–1700		**1525–41** Conquest of Yucatán by the Spaniards **1697** Capture of Tayasal, last independent Maya city, by the Spaniards

LIST OF ILLUSTRATIONS

The following abbreviations have been used: *a* above; *b* below; *c* centre; *l* left; *r* right; Bibl. de l'Ass. Nat. Bibliothèque de l'Assemblée Nationale; Bibl. des Arts Déco. Bibliothèque des Arts Décoratifs; Bibl. Nat. Bibliothèque Nationale; Bibl. Nac. Biblioteca Nacional; MNA Museo Nacional de Antropología

COVER

Front Diego Rivera. *Offering of Fruits, Tobacco, Cacao and Vanilla to the Emperor.* Fresco, 1950. Palacio Nacional, Mexico
Spine Ceremony called *xocotl. Codex Borbonicus.* Bibl. de l'Ass. Nat., Paris

OPENING

1 Cortés is given command of the army. Painting on copper after Antonio de Solis. Museo de America, Madrid
2 Three Spanish soldiers during the first engagements against the Indians of Tabasco. *Ibid.*
3 Soldiers bringing ashore anchors, cables and sails before obeying Cortés' order for his own fleet to be destroyed. *Ibid.*
4 Cortés' first meeting with Moctezuma's envoys. *Ibid.*
5 Cortés entering Tlaxcala. *Ibid.*
6 Cortés meeting Moctezuma II. *Ibid.*
7 Moctezuma pays tribute to Cortés. *Ibid.*
8 The battle of Tepeaca. *Ibid.*

Xochicalco/Tula/Texcocan rulers	Aztecs
650–950 Xochicalco, a rival to Tula, reached its peak between 600 and 800, when the temple of Quetzalcoatl, the Plumed Serpent, was constructed **856** Foundation of Tula by the Toltecs **967** Departure of a group of Toltecs, led by Quetzalcoatl, for Chichén Itzá **1168** Destruction of Tula by the Chichimecs. End of Toltec power	
	1325 The Mexica choose the site of Tenochtitlán as a place to settle **1372–91** Reign of Acamapichtli, leader of the Mexica **1391–1415** Reign of Huitzilíhuitl, leader of the Mexica **1415–26** Reign of Chimalpopoca, leader of the Mexica **1426–40** Reign of Itzcóatl, 4th Mexica sovereign
1409–18 Reign of Ixtlilxóchitl, ruler of Texcoco **1418–72** Reign of Nezahualcóyotl	**1428** Decisive victory of the Mexica over their neighbours. Formation of Triple Alliance between the Mexica, the Texcocans and the Tacubans **1440–68** Reign of Moctezuma I, father of the Aztec empire **1468–81** Reign of Axayácatl **1481–6** Reign of Tízoc
1472–1515 The son of Nezahualcóyotl, Nezahualpilli, retains a strong role for Texcoco in the Triple Alliance through his wisdom and skill	**1486–1502** Reign of Ahuítzotl and extension of the empire's frontiers **1487** Consecration of the Great Temple in Tenochtitlán **1500** Flooding of Tenochtitlán **1502–20** Reign of Moctezuma II and consolidation of the empire
1515–20 Reign of Cacama, nephew of Moctezuma II	**1519** Moctezuma II learns that Cortés has disembarked **1520** Moctezuma II dies, a prisoner of Cortés. Retreat of the *Noche Triste*
1520–1 Reign of Cacamatzin **1521–31** Fernando Ixtlilxóchitl, one of Nezahualpilli's sons, supports Cortés	**1520** Brief reign of Cuitláhuac **1520–5** Reign of Cuauhtémoc **1521** Fall of Tenochtitlán; the city is sacked **1525** Death of Cuauhtémoc and collapse of Aztec empire

9 Cortés takes Moctezuma II prisoner. *Ibid.*
11 Quetzalcoatl. *Codex Telleriano-Remensis.* Bibl. Nat., Paris

CHAPTER 1

12 Flyleaf of Diego Durán's manuscript, *Historia de las Indias de Nueva España*, 1581. Bibl. Nac., Madrid
13 Aztec sculpture of man's head. MNA, Mexico City
14 Sculpture of the Toltec period from Tula. MNA, Mexico City
15a Maize cultivation. *Codex Florentino*
15b Migration of the Mexica. Drawing from *Codex Azcatitlan.* Bibl. Nat., Paris
16 Camaxtli, god of the north, of hunting and of war. Drawing in Diego Durán, op. cit.
17a Aztec statue of Xochipilli, god of flowers, love,

dancing and poetry. MNA, Mexico
17b War between the ancient Mexican peoples. *Codex Telleriano-Remensis.* Bibl. Nat., Paris
18 The gods Huitzilopochtli, Tezcatlipoca, Tlaloc and Paynal. *Codex Florentino*
19 The seven legendary caves. Drawing in Mexican manuscript. Bibl. Nat., Paris
20a The migration of the Mexica. Drawing from an illustrated manuscript. Bibl. Nat., Paris
20–1 Foundation of Tenochtitlán. *Codex Azcatitlan.* Bibl. Nat., Paris
22 The cactus and the serpent. *Codex Florentino*
22–3 The emblem of the foundation of Tenochtitlán – the eagle on the cactus devouring a serpent – in Diego Durán, op. cit.
23 Transportation of blocks of stone by the Mexica. Drawing in Diego Durán, op. cit.

24 Fish from the lake of the Valley of Mexico. Drawings in *Codex Florentino*

24–5 The system of using *chinampas*. Anonymous painting. Museo de la Ciudad, Mexico

26 Native lord. *Codex Ixtlilxóchitl*. Bibl. Nat., Paris

27 Types of tribute paid to the monarchs. Drawings from an illustrated manuscript. Bibl. Nat., Paris

28*l* Working in gold and silver. *Codex Florentino*

28*r* Gold pectoral from tomb 7, Monte Albán. Museo Regional de Oaxaca, Mexico

29 Gold mask of the god Xipe Totec from tomb 7, Monte Albán. *Ibid.*

CHAPTER 2

30 Tlaloc, god of rain. *Codex Ixtlilxóchitl*

31 Aztec calendar stone

32*l* Crickets of the Valley of Mexico. *Codex Florentino*

32*r* Calendar of the fifty-two-year cycle. *Ibid.*

33 The fire ceremony. *Codex Borbonicus*. Bibl. de l'Ass. Nat., Paris

34 Ceremony called *xocotl. Ibid.*

35 Ball game known as *tlachtli. Ibid.*

36 Map depicting human sacrifices, 1550. Archives of the Indies, Seville

37 Warriors' armour. *Codex Florentino*

38*l* One of Moctezuma's treasures. Museum für Völkerkunde, Vienna

38*r* Aztec prince in his finery. Drawing in Diego Durán, op. cit.

39 Featherworkers. *Codex Florentino*

40 Human sacrifice in Diego Durán, op. cit.

41 Battle between Aztecs and their neighbours. *Ibid.*

43*a* Battle between Aztecs and their neighbours, *Ibid.*

43*b* Eagle-knights and jaguar-knights. *Codex Ixtlilxóchitl*

44 Nezahualcóyotl, ruler of Texcoco. *Ibid.*

45 Objects of tribute. *Codex Mendoza*, 1541–2. British Museum, London

CHAPTER 3

46 J. Chapman. Human sacrifice on the *teocalli*. Engraving

47 Plan of the city of Mexico. Anonymous, 17th century. Bibl. des Arts Déco., Paris

48*r* Portrait of Axayácatl. Anonymous painting. Österreichische Nationalbibliothek, Vienna

49*a* Verico. *Aztec High Priest Plucks the Heart from a Sacrificial Victim*. 19th-century hand-coloured print

49*b* Cannibalism. Drawing in *Codex Magliabecchiano*. Library of the Musée de l'Homme, Paris

50–1 Mexico and its surroundings. French engravings of the late 17th century

52–3 Combat between gladiators. Italian engraving, c. 1820. Bibl. des Arts Déco., Paris

53 Cannibalism. *Codex Florentino*

54*a* Human sacrifice. *Codex Magliabecchiano*

54*b* Sacrificial knife

55 Priest offering the heart of a sacrificed man to the gods. 19th-century engraving in Désiré Charnay, *Les anciennes Villes du nouveau monde*. Library of the Musée de l'Homme, Paris

56 The *teocalli* of Mexico. Italian engraving, c. 1820

57 Reign of Ahuítzotl. *Codex Telleriano-Remensis*

58–9*a* Map of Mexico and surrounding lagoons. Giovanni Francesco Gemelli-Careri, *A Voyage round the World*, 1719. Bibl. Nat., Paris

58–9*b* Bird's-eye view of Mexico. Anonymous 17th-century engraving. Bibliothèque Service Historique de la Marine, Vincennes

60 Nezahualpilli, ruler of Texcoco. *Codex Ixtlilxóchitl*

61 Symbols designating the days of a divinatory calendar. *Codex Magliabecchiano*

62 Portrait of Moctezuma II. Bibl. Nac., Mexico

63 The seats of power in Moctezuma's time. Drawing in Thomas Gage, *History of the Mexican Empire*. Library of the Musée de l'Homme, Paris

64–5 Diego Rivera. *Great Tenochtitlán: The Sale of Maize* (detail). Fresco, 1945. Palacio Nacional, Mexico

66–7 Diego Rivera. *The Market of Tenochtitlán: Manufacture of Mosaic and Golden Jewelry under the Zapotec Civilization*. Fresco, 1942. *Ibid.*

68–9 Diego Rivera. *Offering of Fruits, Tobacco, Cacao and Vanilla to the Emperor*. Fresco, 1950. *Ibid.*

70–1 Panorama of the valley of the lakes and of Great Tenochtitlán at the start of the 17th century. Fresco after Andrés de Covarrubias. Museo de la Ciudad, Mexico

71*b* Ceremony. *Codex Magliabecchiano*

CHAPTER 4

72 Hernán Cortés and his army entering the city of Tlaxcala. Anonymous painting. Museo de America, Madrid

73 Portrait of Hernán Cortés. After Jaldana Maestro. Museo Nacional de Historia, Mexico

74–5 Moctezuma sees the comet. Drawing in Diego Durán, op. cit.

75 Organization of the divinatory calendar by Oxomoco and Cipactonal. *Codex Borbonicus*

76–7 Moctezuma is informed in a dream, by Nezahualpilli, of the destruction of the Triple Alliance. Anonymous engraving, 1518

77*r* Signs of the divinatory calendar. *Codex Florentino*

78*a* Battle between Spaniards and Aztecs. *Codex Lienzo de Tlaxcala*. Bibl. Nat., Paris

78–9 Feather headdress from the treasures that Cortés received from Moctezuma II. Museum für Völkerkunde, Vienna

79 Offerings made to Hernán Cortés and Marina, also known as Malinche. *Codex Lienzo de Tlaxcala*

80*l* Hernán Cortés meets the Indians from the Tlaxcalan region. Illustration in Diego Durán, op. cit.

80–1 The meeting of Cortés and Moctezuma. Italian engraving, c. 1820

82–3 Monleon. Hernán Cortés orders the destruction

of his own fleet. Painting. Naval Museum, Madrid
84–5 Miguel Gonzalez. Cortés being welcomed by
Moctezuma II. Series of paintings, 1698. Museo de
America, Madrid
86–7*a* The Aztecs in battle with the Spaniards.
Drawing in Diego Durán, op. cit.
86–7*b* Battle between Spaniards and Aztecs. *Codex
Lienzo de Tlaxcala*
88 Hernán Cortés has a small fleet constructed.
Drawing in Diego Durán, op. cit.
88–9 Battle of Otumba, 8 July 1520. Lithograph in
Histoire d'Amérique latine et des Antilles 1500–1534,
1645. Bibl. Nat., Paris

CHAPTER 5

90 Plan of the city of Tenochtitlán. 16th-century
engraving. Museo de la Ciudad, Mexico
91 Torture by savage dogs. Bibl. Nat., Paris
92–3 Cortés puts an end to human sacrifices.
Lithograph in *Histoire d'Amérique latine et des Antilles
1500–1534*, 1645. *Ibid.*
93*b* Cortés and his army break the idols. *Ibid.*
94*l* Former Aztec practices. Drawing in *Codex
Florentino*
94*r* Don Pedro Moya de Contreras. Drawing in
D. Vicente Riva Palacia, *Mexico a través de los siglos*.
Library of the Institut des Hautes Etudes d'Amérique
latine, Paris
95 Miguel Gonzalez. The Aztec nobles are converted
to Christianity. 1698. Museo de America, Madrid
96 The Spanish army destroys the Aztecs' idols. *Ibid.*
97*a* Baptism of the lords of Tlaxcala. *Codex Lienzo
de Tlaxcala*
97*b* First Christian church built at Texcoco.
Engraving in D. Vicente Riva Palacia, op. cit.
98–9 Miguel Gonzalez. *Baptism of the Aztecs*.
Painting, 1698. Museo de America, Madrid
99*a* Raising the cross in an Aztec town
100*a* The lord of Tabasco offers native women
to Cortés, c. 1820. Italian engraving
100*b* Cortés and his mistress Marina. Anonymous
painting. Museo de America, Madrid
102–3 Detail from a book of accounts. *Codex
Gobernadores*. Bibl. Nac., Madrid
103 Diego Muñoz Canargo. 16th-century coat of
arms of Spain in D. Vicente Riva Palacia, op. cit.
104 Juan Gerson. *Apocalypse of Tecamachalco*. 1850.
Private collection
105 Cultivation of gardens established in marshes.
Drawing from a manuscript of 1554 with Mexican
pictographs and Spanish text. Library of the Musée
de l'Homme, Paris
106–7 Governors, viceroys and lords of Tlaxcala
under Charles V's coat of arms, 1550–64. *Codex
Lienzo de Tlaxcala*
107*b* Victim of an epidemic treated with potions.
Codex Florentino

CHAPTER 6

108 Portrait of half-breeds. 18th-century Mexican
painting. Museo de America, Madrid
109 Andrés Garcia. Carmelita. 19th-century statue.
Museo de America, Madrid
110 Portrait of a noble. Drawing in *Codex
Postcolombino-Indigena*. Museo de America,
Madrid
111 The palace of Virreyes. 16th-century anonymous
painted screen. Museo de America, Madrid
112–3 Juan G. de Trasmonte. Bird's-eye view of the
city of Mexico. 1628. Museo de la Ciudad, Mexico
114–5 Cuvillier. Mexico cathedral from the Plaza
Mayor. Lithograph in Carl Nebel, *Voyage pittoresque
et archéologique dans la partie la plus intéressante du
Mexique*, 1836. Bibl. Nat., Paris
116 Luis de Mena. *The Different Races Established
since the Spanish Conquest*. 16th–century painting.
Museo de America, Madrid
117 J. Michaud and Thomas. Preparation of tortillas.
Lithograph, 1847. Bibl. Nac., Mexico
118 The Indian as beast of burden. Anonymous
engraving, 1811
119 Spanish *haciendas* and settlements of San Andrés
Chalchicomula. Late 17th-century anonymous
engraving. Private collection
120*a* Primitivo Miranda. *Holy week at Cuautitlán*.
Early 19th–century painting. Chapultepec Museum,
Mexico
120–1 *Half-breeds*. Anonymous 18th-century
Mexican painting. Museo Nacional de Historia,
Mexico
122*a* Aquita Arrieta. *Pulquería*. 19th-century
painting. Chapultepec Museum, Mexico
122*b* Eduardo Piagret. *Mexican Kitchen*. Painting,
1856. *Ibid.*
123 Lemercier. Indians on the way to market.
Lithograph in Carl Nebel, op. cit.
124*a* Textile patterns. Private collection
124–5 *Half-breeds at the market*. 18th-century
Mexican painting. Museo de America, Madrid
126–7 Fr. Miathe. Tampico. Lithograph in Carl
Nebel, op. cit.
128 Miguel Cabrera. Indians. 18th-century painting.
Museo de America, Madrid

DOCUMENTS

130 Calendar drawn on agave paper. Library of
the Musée de l'Homme, Paris
131 18th-century codex of the sun depicting the
cult of Tonatiuh. Bibl. Nat., Paris
132 Page of the *tonalamatl* or divinatory calendar.
Drawing in *Codex Borbonicus*
133 The fire relit in the temple. Drawing in *Codex
Magliabecchiano*
134–5 Migration of the ancient Mexican people.

Drawing in Giovanni Francesco Gemelli-Careri, op. cit.

136 Patrick Mérienne. The Mexica migration from Tula to Tenochtitlán. Map

138 Tzapotla Tena. *Codex Florentino*

139 Agave in Giovanni Francesco Gemelli-Careri, op. cit.

140 Teaching of children and adolescents. Engraving in *Codex Mendoza*

141 Page of the *tonalamatl* depicting Tlaloc. *Codex Telleriano-Remensis*

142 Quetzalcoatl. Drawing in *Codex Massicano Vaticano*. Gallimard collection

143 Bernard Picart. Offerings to Quetzalcoatl. 19th-century engraving. Bibl. des Arts Déco., Paris

144 Temple of Tlahuizcalpantecuhtli at Tula

145 Two-headed serpent

146 and 147 Different types of tribute. Engravings in Don Francisco Antonio Lorenzana, *Historia de Nueva España*, 1770. Bibl. Nat., Paris.

148 Butterfly. *Codex Florentino*

149 Different sorts of tribute in Don Francisco Antonio Lorenzana, op. cit.

151 Merchants of the pre-hispanic era. *Codex Florentino*

152 Market at Tlatelolco in 1500. 18th-century engraving. Mary Evans Picture Library, London

153 Tarascan craftsmanship. Engravings in D. Vicente Riva Palacia, op. cit.

154a Diego Rivera. *The Arts of Tarascan civilization*. Fresco, 1942. Palacio Nacional, Mexico

155 Blacksmiths. Drawing in *Codex Florentino*

156 The stone of sacrifices. Lithograph in Carl Nebel, op. cit.

157 Ignacio Marquina. Reconstruction of the Great Temple of Tenochtitlán. American Museum of Natural History, New York

159 Human sacrifice in Diego Durán op. cit.

161a The stone of sacrifices. Lithograph in Carl Nebel, op. cit.

161b Temple of the sun. Drawing in *Histoire d'Amérique latine et des Antilles 1500–1534*, 1645. Bibl. Nat., Paris

162 Death of Moctezuma II. 18th-century anonymous engraving. Mary Evans Picture Library, London

163 Nezahualpilli announces the Spaniards' arrival to Moctezuma. Mary Evans Picture Library, London

164–5 Meeting between Cortés and Moctezuma. 18th-century engraving. Mary Evans Picture Library, London

166 and 167b Panorama of the Valley of Mexico. 19th-century ink drawing. Bibl. Nat., Paris

167a Patrick Mérienne. The journeys of Cortés from 1519 to 1520. Map

168 The siege of Tenochtitlán. Engraving in D. Vicente Riva Palacia, op. cit.

169 Naval battle on the lagoon of Mexico. Anonymous 18th-century engraving. Mary Evans Picture Library, London

171 Cortés victorious at Tabasco. Lithograph in *Histoire d'Amérique latine et des Antilles 1500–1534*, 1645. Bibl. Nat., Paris

174 Medicinal plants. Drawing in *Codex Florentino*

175 Pulque festival. Drawing in *Codex Magliabecchiano*

176–7 Baptism and funeral. Drawings in *Codex Florentino*

178 Doctor and patient

179 Virgin of Guadalupe. Gallimard collection

180 Title page of *Santa María Totlaconantzin Guadalupe*, 1649. Gallimard collection

181 A 16th-century Mexican church. Gallimard collection

182 Poor quarter in Mexico. Engraving

184–5 Patrick Mérienne. The Aztec empire at the time of the Triple Alliance. Map

INDEX

Figures in italic refer to pages on which captions appear.

A–C

Acamapichtli 23–4
Ahuítzotl 49, 52, 54, 56, 57, *57*, 58, 61
Axayácatl 48, *48*, 85
Cacamatzin 63, 86
Chalca, the *19*, 32, 80, 86
Chalco 17, 45, 63, 80
Charles V 71, *78*, 89, *107*, 166
Cortés, Hernán 58, 73, 75, 77, *78*, 79, 79, 80, *81*, 82, 83, *83*, 84, *84*, 85, *85*, 86, 87, *87*, 88, 89, *89*, 91, 92, *92*, 98, *98*, 99, 101, *101*, 151, 162, 164, *164*, 165, 166–70, *171*
Cuauhtémoc 86, *87*, 89, 98, 99, 168
Cuitláhuac 86, *87*, 98

D–I

Díaz del Castillo, Bernal *73*, *82*, *101*, 151–3
Durán, Diego 13, 60, *76*, 147–50, 162–6
Great Temple 47, 49, *51*, 52, 146, *157*
Huitzilopochtli *18*, 20, 21, *21*, 40, *51*, 53, 77, 84, 86, *141*, 145–7
Itzcóatl 31, 48

M–O

Mexica *13*,*15*,*16*, *17*, 19, 20, 21, *21*, 22, *22*, 23, *23*, 24, 26,

28, 29, 38, 40, 48, 49, 57, 58, 63, 91, 98, 102, *134*
Moctezuma I 31, 32, 37, 38, 39, 43, 45, 47, 48, 49, 57, 145
Moctezuma II 61, 62, *62*, 63, 73, 75, 76, *76*, 77, 78, *78*, 79, 80, *81*, 82, 83, 84, *84*, 85, 86, *87*, 101, *113*, 156, 162, *162*, *163*, 164, *164*, 165, 166
Nezahualcóyotl 29, 39, 43–4, *44*, 47, 58
Nezahualpilli 57, 58,

60, *60*, 75, *76*, 86, *163*
Noche Triste 86, *87*, 88, *89*
Oaxaca, 26, 57, 61, 62

P–Q

Philip II *103*, *115*
Puebla 17, 57, 63, 121
Quetzalcoatl 14, 17, 23, 28, 43, 76, 77, 78, 84, 132, 134, 135, 137, 138, 139, 141–3, *143*, 145

S–T

Sahagún, Bernardino de *53*, *65*, *67*, *69*, *74*, 141–3, 153

Tacuba 28, 29, 52, 57, 83, 84, 101, 165
Tarascans, the 48, 56, 60
Tenochtitlán 20, *21*, 22, *22*, 24, 28, 29, 38, 40, *41*, 42, *42*, 44, 45, 47, 48, 49, *51*, 56, 57, 58, *59*, 63, *65*, *67*, 70, 79, 86, 87, *87*, 89, *91*, 106, 126, 127, *134*, 147, 150, *157*, 166–70, *168*
Teotihuacán 14, 52, 132, 138, 160
Tepanecs, the 19, *19*, 24, 26, 29, 80, 86
Texcocans, the 29, 38, 86, 91
Texcoco 25, 26, 28,

29, 38, 39, 40, 42, 44, *44*, 52, 56, 58, *60*, 63, 83, 84, 86, 97, 98, *163*, 165, 173
Tezcatlipoca *18*, 133, 135
Tízoc 48
Tlacaélel 38, 145–7
Tlaloc *18*, *31*, 134, 135, *141*
Tlatelolco 22, 24, 45, 48, *59*, 86, 104, 126, 151–3, *151*, *152*
Tlaxcala 57, 60, 62, 63, 79, 80, 86, *89*, *97*, 98, *101*, *107*, 110, 146, 156
Tlaxcalans, the 16, 48, 63, 80, *81*, 87, 102,

107
Toci 75, 165
Toltecs, the 14, 15, 16, 17, 18, 19, 24, 25, 28, 76, 94, 127, 142, 144–5, 153–4
Triple Alliance, the *27*, 28, 29, 33, 37, 38, 40 42, 56, 57, 58, 60, 61, 62, 63, 70, 80, 86, 162
Tula 13, 14, 15, 17, 18, 23, 28, 63, 76, 127, 132, 141, 142, 144, *144*, 160

W–Z

War of the Flowers 33, 36, *36*, 62, 145
Zapotecs, the 57, *67*

ACKNOWLEDGMENTS

Grateful acknowledgment is made for permission to use material from the following works: (pp. 130–2, 138–9, 139–41, 144–5, 145–6, 154–5, 171–3) from *Aztec Thought and Culture: A Study of the Ancient Nahuatl Mind* by Miguel León-Portilla, copyright © 1963 by the University of Oklahoma Press, Norman, Oklahoma, USA; (pp. 79, 82, 101, 151–3) from *The Conquest of New Spain* by Bernal Díaz, translated by J. M. Cohen (Penguin Classics, 1963), copyright © J. M. Cohen 1963, reproduced by permission of Penguin Books Ltd, London; (pp. 70, 81, 84, 85, 92, 166–70) from *Hernando Cortés, Letters from Mexico* by A. R. Pagden, editor and translator, translated by A. R. Pagden, translation copyright © 1971 by Anthony Pagden, used by permission of Viking Penguin, a division of Penguin Books USA Inc.; (pp. 172–3, 176–8, 178–81) from *Man-Gods in the Mexican Highlands: Indian Power and Colonial Society, 1520–1800* by Serge Gruzinski, translated by Eileen Corrigan, with the permission of the publishers, Stanford University Press, Stanford, California, USA, © 1989 by the Board of Trustees of the Leland Stanford Junior University. Patrick Mérienne, Paris, drew the maps on pp. 136, 167 and 184–5.

PHOTO CREDITS

All rights reserved 86–7*a*, 142, 154*b*, 163, 181, 182. Artephot Oronoz 43*a*, 72, 82–3, 84–5, 95, 96, 99*a*, 124–5. Artephot/Percheron 75. Arxiu Mas, Madrid 41, 88, 98–9, 100*b*, 102–3, 108, 110, 111, 128. Bibl. de l'Ass. Nat., Paris 33, 34, 35. Bibl. Nat., Paris 11, 15*b*, 17*b*, 19, 20*a*, 20–1, 26, 27, 30, 43*a*, 43*b*, 44, 57, 58–9*a*, 60, 76–7, 77*r*, 88–9, 91, 92–3, 93*b*, 97*a*, 106–7, 114–5, 123, 126–7, 131, 134–5, 139, 141, 146, 147, 156, 161*a*, 161*b*, 166, 167*b*, 169, 171. Bridgeman Art Library, London 45. Bulloz, Paris 143. Chapultepec Museum, Mexico 120*a*, 122*a*, 122*b*. Jean-Loup Charmet 50–1, 52–3, 56, 80–1, 86–7*b*, 100*a*, 175. Dagli-Orti, Paris front cover, 1, 2, 3, 4, 5, 6, 7, 8, 9, 12, 14, 16, 17*a*, 22–3, 23, 24–5, 28*r*, 29, 36, 38*r*, 40, 62, 64–5, 66–7, 68–9, 70–1, 71*b*, 74, 80*l*, 90, 112–3, 117, 144, 154*a*, 159. F. Delebecque 15*a*, 18, 22, 24, 28*l*, 32*l*, 32*r*, 37, 39, 47, 49*b*, 53, 55, 58–9*b*, 61, 63, 75, 94*l*, 94*r*, 97*b*, 103, 104, 105, 107*b*, 119, 124*a*, 130, 132, 133, 138, 140, 148, 153, 155, 168, 174, 176–7, 178. Explorer/C. Lénars 145. Explorer/Sugar 31. Explorer, Paris/Mary Evans Picture Library, London 46, 49*a*, 74–5, 152, 162, 164–5. Giraudon, Paris 13, 73, 120–1. Museo de America, Madrid 109, 116. Museum für Völkerkunde, Vienna 38*l*, 76–7. Nationalbibliothek, Vienna 48*r*. Rota, Library Services of the American Museum of Natural History, New York 157. Scala, Florence 54*a*.

Serge Gruzinski
was born in 1949 in Tourcoing.
Docteur ès Lettres, archivist-palaeographer,
former member of the Ecole Française de Rome
and the Casa de Velasquez,
associate researcher of the Instituto Nacional de Antropología
e Historia de Mexico
through the Ministry of Foreign Affairs (1978–82),
he is currently a researcher with the CNRS,
and is co-director of the Centre de Recherches sur le Mexique,
l'Amérique Centrale et les Andes
(CNRS/Ecole des Hautes Etudes en Sciences Sociales), Paris.
Serge Gruzinski has carried out research in Italy, Spain,
the USA and Mexico, where he lived for seven years.
The author of numerous articles,
his books include
*Man-Gods in the Mexican Highlands:
Indian Power and Colonial Society 1520–1800* (1989)
and *Conquering the Indian Mind: The Making of Colonial Indian
Cultures in Spanish Mexico, 16th–18th Centuries* (1992).

© Gallimard 1987
English translation © Thames and Hudson Ltd, London,
and Harry N. Abrams, Inc., New York, 1992

Translated by Paul G. Bahn

All Rights Reserved. No part of this publication may
be reproduced without prior permission in writing
from the publisher.

Printed and bound in Italy
by Editoriale Libraria, Trieste